ON WITH
THE BUTTER!
Spread More Living
onto Everyday Life

HEIDI HERMAN

On With the Butter!
Spread More Living onto Everyday Life

Cover design by Kelly A. Martin
DepositPhotos: Galyna, Teploleta
Book design and production by F + P Graphic Design
Editing by Windword Literary Services

Copyright © 2020 by Heidi Herman
V1.0 r1.0

Although the author and publisher have made every effort to ensure
that the information in this book was correct at press time, the author and
publisher do not assume and hereby disclaim any liability to any party for any loss,
damage, or disruption caused by errors or omissions, whether such errors or omissions
result from negligence, accident, or any other cause.

This publication is meant as a source of valuable information for the reader; however,
it is not meant as a substitute for direct expert assistance. If such level of assistance
is required, the services of a competent professional should be sought.
This book is not intended as a substitute for the medical advice of physicians.
The reader should regularly consult a physician in matters relating to his/her health
and particularly with respect to any symptoms that may require diagnosis or medical attention

All rights reserved. No part of this book may be reproduced or transmitted in any form
or by any means, electronic or mechanical, to include photocopying, recording,
or by any informational storage or retrieval system, without the written permission
of the author, except where permitted by law.

First Edition

ISBN: 978-1-947233-03-4
Hekla Publishing and the Hekla logo are trademarks
belonging to Hekla Publishing LLC

Inspiration & Appreciation

I have many people to thank for the inspiration and development of this book.

My mom, who was an inspiration to so many people, simply through her vitality and continual zest for living. She had a passion for life until the day of her passing at the age of ninety-four. To me, she was a mentor, a teacher, a cohort, and a friend.

The amazing group of people in my life who have been supportive and have had a profound impact on my view of the world: Emily K., Mike K., Dorothy, Sunna, KC, Jennifer, and Pam.

My husband, Raymond, who supports my dreams and helps me through all the ups and downs of the book-writing process.

My fellow writers and authors who provided support, encouragement, feedback, and more than a little brain-storming.

The team at Windword Literary Service for their invaluable assistance: my amazing developmental editor and writing coach, Toni Robino, who helped me through the process of putting this book together and helped me clarify the message I wanted to share; and Doug Wagner, with his knowledge, input, and support in the arduous editing process that helped make me a better writer.

IV ON WITH THE BUTTER!

Contents

Introduction

"Not what we have but what we enjoy
constitutes our abundance."
—Epicurus, Greek philosopher

O*n with the butter* (Áfram með smjörið) is an old
Icelandic expression that means "carry on," "keep
doing what you're doing," "forge ahead," or "keep moving."

That sentiment was one of the countless things I learned
from my vivacious Icelandic mother. "Just keep moving"
was her favorite mantra. She taught me by example to
embrace life and live in the moment. I have witnessed
firsthand how people respond to that ideal and how they
became motivated to do more themselves. Now that I
know it's something that many people strive to achieve,
I'm even more grateful that this spirit is engrained in me.

We've all heard the popular expression YOLO—you only live once. We're reminded to take advantage of the days we're given, but how exactly do we do that?

Some people focus on finding happiness, and while that's not a bad idea, the definition of happiness is different for everyone, so we have to figure out what makes us happy. To do that, we need to experience life in all its glory—the exciting and the mundane, the good and the bad, the happy and the sad. The search might lead to peace and contentment, purposefulness, action and excitement, higher knowledge, or caretaking.

We all seek these things to one degree or another, but there's often one desire that becomes the primary focus. Before retirement, that focus is often our job or career. But after we retire, we discover that life changes and our primary focus seems to disappear. And that's when the exploration begins again. That's when we find new things that challenge us or just make us smile.

As we get older, it's easy to become consumed with our health and taking care of ourselves. We may change our diet, take prescriptions to treat medical conditions, and focus more on physical fitness. But while we're working so hard to increase our life span, what are we doing to appreciate and make the most of that time? Those are the questions *On with the Butter* invites us to entertain.

There are many books that offer advice on how to live healthier, how to be happier, how to age with grace and become physically fit. But while they're all worthwhile pursuits, I'd always felt like one was missing. I now know that it's the philosophy that my mom instilled in me—the curiosity and desire to experience life and the creativity to find many ways to do it.

I thought of Mom as a life adventurer. She taught me to embrace life with exuberance. Well into her nineties, she inspired those around her simply by the way she lived. She was constantly active: writing books, traveling, visiting friends and family, and living each day to the fullest. And she was just one of the great role models I was blessed to have. My father, who had his own version of living every day to the fullest, was another. He'd dropped out of high school, lied about his age to join the U.S. Navy, and was stationed in Iceland before his nineteenth birthday. Although he never had any higher learning or formal education, he became an ordained minister, general contractor, and self-taught architect. To me, he was a brilliant thinker and problem-solver.

So after Dad was diagnosed with stage three esophageal cancer, I was staggered. I struggled to accept that the larger-than-life dynamo had been knocked down to life-size. I was forty-six at the time, and as I watched one of my heroes undergo surgery, radiation, and chemotherapy in an aggressive battle to survive, my commitment to making the most of my own life became stronger. For six months, he fought to stay alive, and shortly after he turned eighty-nine, we got the incredible news that his cancer was in full remission. The energy that Dad had put into healing was now channeled into living, and it gave me a different perspective. I had always thought life is too short to be taken for granted, but I realized that life is also far too long to be squandered on unhappiness or boredom.

Although my life was full and I was content, I wanted to experience more. I wanted to revisit some of the things I once enjoyed and try things that I never thought I'd try. Thanks to my role models, I'd always been a "doer," but my new view of life made me realize that I had also let a lot of fun opportunities pass me by. And I decided to stop that. I decided to take the "on with the butter" approach to my everyday life. And after I retired, instead of buying a rocking chair, I learned to fly.

My sincere hope is that this book, which is packed with ideas for embracing life with zest and exuberance, will arm you with what you need to do just that. You don't have to live every day to the fullest, but I'm challenging you to live fully every day, whatever that means to you.

On with the butter!

1

Just Say Yes

opportunities are endless

"The true enjoyments must be spontaneous
and compulsive and look to no remoter end."
—C.S. Lewis, author of *The Chronicles of Narnia*

Whether we're nine years old or ninety, taking advantage of spur-of-the-moment invitations and opportunities adds a slice of unexpected fun and adventure to everyday life. Being spontaneous—even occasionally—also prevents us from getting into ruts and opens the door to more connection with our family and friends. And it turns out that playing life by ear can be beneficial for our health and happiness.

Fun surprises turn on "connector emotions" like love and joy that tell our brains to release "happy hormones." That makes anxiety and stress go down, which in turn helps to lower our risk for heart disease and high blood pressure. In other words, welcoming unplanned adventures is good therapy for us. I can almost hear my fellow planners groaning, but don't worry—I'm not suggesting that you trash your appointment book or turn your routine upside down. I'm just challenging you to enjoy unexpected opportunities when they present themselves.

It's not unusual for people to become less spontaneous and follow a more rigid schedule as we get older. But becoming regimented is not a requirement of aging, and I don't recommend it. I'm convinced that my mom's "Just say yes" philosophy contributed to her youthful vitality. And that way of living didn't stop once she entered her eighties or even her nineties. That's how Mom once ended up on a dance floor hopping and flapping her "wings" along with twenty other people while I looked on, grinning. We were at the Yuma (Arizona) Civic Center for the Scandinavian

Festival hosted by the Sons of Norway Sola Lodge when I heard the unmistakable tune of the Chicken Dance. I turned to my mom. "Oh, we have to watch," I said. "I love this!"

An announcement came over the PA system that anyone who wanted to learn the Chicken Dance should gather on the dance floor.

"Did they say *Chicken* Dance?" she said, sounding almost horrified. "What is that?" Clearly, she was imagining the worst.

"Seriously?" I said, grabbing her hand. "Then you have to learn. It will be a hoot."

That settled it. In Mom's mind, there was no higher praise for something enjoyable than calling it a "hoot." She motioned for me to go with her, but I shook my head, holding up my phone. "I have to stay here and take pictures for your Instagram." When she hesitated, I nodded and smiled encouragingly. A true Viking, Mom wasn't about to back down from a new adventure, so she gamely trotted onto the polished wood floor and took a place right in front of the instructor. And she held her own, too, at least until the music sped up and she was giggling so much that she gave up on the steps and just flapped her arms. She had such a good time that I decided to say yes to a traditional Norwegian group dance that reminded me of the square dancing I'd learned in elementary school. Since everyone was learning at the same time, my missteps would blend in with everyone else's. It looked like so much fun that I was willing to jump in beside her.

Even though "Just say yes" was part of Mom's philosophy of life, she was still self-conscious at times. It's easier to take the risk of looking silly when you have someone familiar doing it with you. And in this case, being her sidekick was as good for me as it was for her.

Planned Spontaneity
it's not an oxymoron

"If there's one thing I learned,
it's that nobody is here forever.
You have to live for the moment,
each and every day ...
the here, the now."
—Simone Elkeles, American author

It may sound like a contradiction, but we can plan to be more spontaneous by adding time cushions to our schedules and designating days or time windows for spur-of-the-moment activities and adventures. For example, if it will take ten minutes to pick up your library books, plan thirty minutes or even an hour just in case something is happening when you get there, like a ukulele circle that entertains patrons on Tuesday nights. Who knew?

We've all stumbled upon interesting and entertaining scenes that looked like fun—if only we had the time. How often do we encounter a novel opportunity or see an ad for something unusual but pass it up because we don't have time for it? When was the last time you ran into a friend and didn't say you had too many things to do and places to be to grab a cup of coffee? Instead of wishing we had more time for spontaneous fun, why not look for opportunities to make that happen?

In addition to adding time cushions to our schedules and designating time for playing it by ear, we can make room for spontaneity in our bigger plans, including celebrations and traveling. So when I was invited to present my children's program "Trolls & Legends of Iceland" at ScanFest, a large Scandinavian festival held every year on the East Coast, I wondered if it might be an opportunity to schedule in some time for unplanned adventures.

Mom and I loved events like these and usually participated by giving presentations and setting up a vendor booth to talk to festival-goers about Icelandic culture and promote our books, and while I was excited about the opportunity to share folklore from the children's stage, a four-day round-trip drive seemed excessive for a one-day event. But since we needed to transport boxes filled with our books, a tent for our outdoor vendor booth, our custom-made six-foot head-in-the-hole Viking photo board, and my Viking-style costume, driving was truly our only option. What to do?

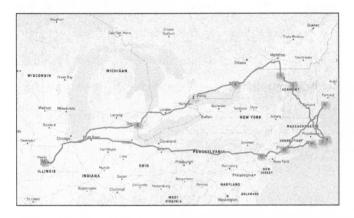

Well, we decided to turn the drive there into a ten-day adventure. Instead of taking the 875-mile direct route, we charted a route from Illinois to New Jersey by way of Canada. It was a perfect opportunity for some scenic and leisurely exploration, and we were excited to visit a few places we hadn't been before. Our route stretched across thirteen states and two Canadian provinces—over two thousand miles—including a stay in Cape Cod, where we rented a condo and took day trips throughout the Northeast before heading to the festival.

While driving through Vermont on the way to Cape Code one afternoon, we were enjoying the warm August temperatures, the green rolling hills, and the local flavors when we encountered an unexpected flavor. Along a two-lane country road we spotted a sign that read "Free Wine Tasting," with an arrow pointing left.

I looked over at Mom. "What do you think?"

She pointed to the left. "Just say yes, Heidi!"

We were both laughing as I drove the quarter-mile to the huge red barn that housed the Boyden Valley Winery. On both sides of the barn, orderly rows of grapevines reached over the hill and extended to the edge of a deciduous forest that met the pale blue sky. This spur-of-the-moment pit stop was already worth it simply for the view.

As we walked inside, we were greeted with upbeat polka music and smiles from the sommelier, Jamie, as she welcomed us to the tasting room, which had a bar that ran the length of one wall and a high ceiling with exposed wood beams. Sunlight streamed through the high windows and reflected off the wine bottles displayed on the shelves lining the walls. Mom and I exchanged a smile. Everything about this place was fun.

We learned that it was Jamie's first season at the winery, but she was highly knowledgeable about the wines and directed us through the tasting like a pro. Tapping our feet to the lively polka music as we sampled a few varieties of wine, we agreed that we liked the gløgg the most. Gløgg is a traditional Scandinavian spiced wine typically made for the winter holidays, and Mom said this version reminded her of the gløgg her grandfather used to serve. I could tell from the smile on her face that it was a happy memory for her.

We were still smiling and tapping our feet when the door opened and two couples walked in and joined us at the bar. They were touring the northeastern United States and had seen the same winery sign that we had. Within minutes, we were chatting like old friends, and after one of the men noticed that Mom was bobbing her head to the music, he held out his hand and invited her to dance. True to form, she said yes without hesitation. They put the spacious barn floor to good use and finished the polka with a flourish of laughter—a beautiful display of living in the moment.

A straight route may be the shortest distance between two points, but a road that twists and curves offers surprises at every turn.

THE CHALLENGE

PRACTICE SAYING YES

"You must live in the present,
launch yourself on every wave,
ind your eternity in each moment."
—Henry David Thoreau, American philosopher

When we talk about being spontaneous or living in the moment, it can even sound frivolous. But practicing being spontaneous has practical purposes, too. It helps us to be more flexible and resilient when things don't go as planned—two qualities we can't do well without.

CHALLENGE CHECKLIST

☐ Pad your schedule with extra time for unexpected activities.

☐ Designate at least one day a month to playing life by ear.

☐ When you get invited to something you're not sure you'll enjoy, say yes anyway.

☐ Recruit a sidekick—or several!

☐ Practice saying yes to invitations.

☐ Notice billboards and take time to check events/locations that seem interesting.

☐ Share my "Just Say Yes" moments on your Facebook page or other social media.

☐ Be a follower on someone else's adventure— say yes when you're invited.

☐ Go to a school event to support children's programs—for your grandchildren or someone else's.

☐ Watch for signs for wine and food tastings, open houses, poetry readings, etc.

☐ Jot events on your calendar as you hear about them.

☐ If someone says, "We should do that," don't just say, "Sure we should." Make a solid plan.

☐ Include time for spontaneity in celebrations and travel plans.

2

Use Innovation

the tools are at your fingertips

"If you always do what you've always done,
you always get what you've always gotten."
—Henry Ford, American industrialist and businessman

Let's face it—change can be hard. But there are times when change is good, like when new technology changes how we connect with each other and the world. We used to hand-write letters and the Postal Service would take days to deliver them, but now we have instant transmission through email. Instead of personal visits, we rely more on telephone conversation and, more recently, live video interactions. Advances in technology aren't limited to social media or electronic communication, computers, tablets, and smartphones offer us an abundance of new activities, experiences, and opportunities for learning, keeping us both mentally and physically active. And it's not just for young people—more than 50 percent of all seniors have smartphones, and almost 75 percent have access to the Internet.

Naturally, we all want to feel comfortable with these innovations. We want to be proficient with the tools and understand how they work. But sometimes that can be difficult. New technology is created every day, so it's not surprising that many of us struggle to keep up with what's out there and how to use it. But the rewards are so great that it's well worth the effort.

Technology makes keeping in touch easier

I created a Facebook account in September 2009 after my mom invited me to join so we could share photos. She was eighty-four years old and wanted to stay connected with her ten children, eighteen grandchildren, and ten-plus great-grandchildren. For the next ten years, Mom stayed active on Facebook, connecting with friends and family, keeping up on the news, and looking at photos from events she couldn't attend in person.

One of the ways she connected was to put all the news she had collected from family members, along with details of her own life, into one long monthly email like a newsletter. She called it *Chatter,* and it helped us all stay up-to-date with each other, even those who didn't follow social media. I think it also helped Mom stay sharp by allowing her to use her writing skills and leverage technology in a way that was faster and easier. If she'd had to type or hand-write individual letters, I imagine we would have gotten far fewer family updates!

While technological innovations have made connecting easier, keeping in touch can still be more difficult today than in generations past. Work schedules aren't always eight to five, weekends are no longer reserved for family time, and grandparents don't always live in the same town—sometimes not even in the same time zone. So embracing the alternatives provided by technology to stay close to our friends and loved ones can help. Among the most popular alternatives are:

- *Facebook.* You can see photos and read posts about events or opinions. You can post a reply hours or even days later. Sometimes simply reading through someone's older posts can help you catch up on their lives.

- *Instant message, text, and email.* You don't have to arrange a convenient time for a phone call or worry that you're interrupting. Instant messages and texts are efficient for quick contact, whereas emails are better-suited for longer communications. Emails can include all the detail and personal thought we once poured onto stationery, but they can be easier to complete and give us the advantage of faster delivery. For people who struggle with arthritis, typing also may be less painful than writing long-hand.

- *Real-time video.* Services like Skype, Zoom, and, Facetime allow us to have personal, face-to-face connections. Communicating with family by way of a smartphone, tablets, or computers can feel more personal when you see them along with hearing them. A smile in a photo can warm your heart, but nothing can take the place of seeing that smiling face and hearing their laughter at the same time.

Stay Informed: News on Demand

For years, we read the morning paper over coffee at the breakfast table. Nowadays, it seems everything has gone digital. Newspaper circulation is down. Some publications have gone to weekly printings while others have increased their rates to stay profitable. In some cases, the online digital version is the only format available.

But online newspapers aren't the only way to stay informed. You can still read the daily edition of your favorite newspaper, but there are other avenues for reading material you might enjoy, courtesy of your computer or smart devices:

- *Blogs.* A blog is an online journal with regular articles posted about a particular topic or theme. Blog topics can range from nutrition and aging to books, wine, and even quilt-making. If you have an interest or passion, it's likely that someone has a blog devoted to it. You can find blogs using your favorite online search engine or a blog listing service like Blogarama, or you can ask for referrals from friends.

- *Newsletters.* Sign up for newsletters from a local organization, a social group, or your favorite author. Electronic newsletters are delivered right to your email on a regular basis; it may vary from weekly to monthly or even quarterly. The best part is, they're usually free and you can cancel anytime.

- *Ebooks and ezines.* Like traditional publications, electronic versions of books and magazines are available to check out free of charge from local libraries. You can also purchase from online sources such as Amazon, Barnes & Noble, and Apple to add to your personal collection.

Find Events and Activities

I love festivals. Strawberry festivals, Pumpkin Days, artists and crafters expos—I'm always on the lookout for the next fun event. I used to have to scour local newspapers and keep a sharp eye out for fliers on community bulletin boards, but many promoters and event coordinators now use social media and online services to advertise events, making it much easier to find out what's going on in the community—or even across the globe.

Today, we can use technology to find events and other opportunities that allow us to connect with the real world. For example, Facebook provides a platform for promoting events. Have you ever noticed the calendar icon and the word *events* on Facebook and wondered what it was? If you haven't, look for it the next time you log on. It's probably on the left, under the word *explore*. When you click on it, you can see all the local events that have been posted. Many are open to the public, and most are free. If you're looking for something to do, this is an excellent place to start.

Ticketing services are another resource for finding events in your area. Ticketmaster, Goldstar, and Eventful are online services where you can purchase tickets for the theater, concerts, or symphony performances. You can access these sites for free, search through the listings for the perfect event, and click on a link to buy tickets.

The website Eventbrite allows organizers to promote events such as local festivals, art shows, family events, and expos. There are a wide variety of events listed, and most don't require an advance ticket. Best of all, many of the events listed on this site are free to attend.

Deep discounts are the next best thing to free. At online coupon sites like Groupon and Social Living, you can find services, events, and activities that are discounted up to 70 percent or more. Since many telephone companies have stopped printing and distributing phone books, most of us no longer have the yellow pages to flip through. It used to be you could look up miniature golf or theaters, but since that resource is gone, local entertainment businesses have turned to new avenues of marketing.

Today, many businesses use coupon promotional sites to advertise their service. Groupon and Social Living allow you to filter by geographical region and select categories such as "health and fitness," "activities," and "things to do." These sites often list activities that aren't widely promoted elsewhere. Ready to try wine and painting, indoor skydiving, virtual reality, concerts at the zoo, or something else that you never even knew existed?

Actively Interact When You Can't Leave Home

With the resources made available by technology, if you can't leave the house, you can still have fun and interact with people around the world. There are hundreds of games online that you can play alone or with other players. Here are some of the games you can play without leaving home:

- Electronic versions of word games such as Scrabble and Boggle that can be downloaded to your phone or tablet

- Electronic versions of board games like chess, checkers, and even Risk. Free games are available from many sites. One example is *https://www.arkadium.com/free-online-games/*

- Puzzles of all types, from crosswords to Sudoku, and games of matching and colors

- Sports such as tennis, boxing, and bowling through home gaming systems like Nintendo, Wii, and Xbox

- Brain games designed specifically to challenge the mind by posing questions and presenting equations and puzzles to solve

Better Fitness through Technology

When we think about fitness, we may have unpleasant flashbacks of doing calisthenics in the high school gymnasium. Or we may think about the gym membership we purchased and how rarely we managed to squeeze in workouts between professional obligations and family time. Thankfully, technology has brought improvements to this area of our lives as well.

Instructor-led exercise routines have been available for years through VHS and DVD technology, and now we can use our computers or tablets to access the same type of exercise routines through videos, many of them available free. You can also search for specific types of workouts such as chair yoga, which was designed for seniors, and use your computer or tablet to follow along, just like watching on your television.

The screen on a smartphone may be too small to easily follow an exercise video, but our phones can still help with fitness. We can download fitness apps (an abbreviation for *applications*) made for our wireless devices. There are many available, some free and others that have a monthly cost. Some automatically count our steps for the day, track our heart rate, and let us keep track of the calories we burn and what we eat. Unfortunately, to count steps and track fitness details, we have to keep our devices with us all the time, but an alternative is wearable technology that looks like a bracelet, such as FitBit, Garmin, and Vivosmart. Similar to the smartphone apps, wearable technology can track steps, calories burned, heart rate, and sleep quality. Smartwatches can do all that *and* tell you the time.

Choosing a program with the features you want and the technology that works for your lifestyle can help you track daily activity and give you the information you need to make healthy choices.

"Science and technology revolutionize our lives, but memory, tradition and myth frame our response." —Arthur Schlesinger, historian

Innovations of the past two centuries have created an environment of convenience and automation. Many tasks can now be done while literally sitting on the couch in our living room. And while these advances can contribute to a sedentary lifestyle that leads to listlessness, we can choose to use technology to add more stimulation and entertainment to our lives instead. It's all a matter of how we use the tools we have at our disposal.

THE CHALLENGE
CONNECT WITH TECHNOLOGY

"Technology is best when it brings people together."
—Matt Mullenweg, American entrepreneur

When we think about technology, it's easy to focus on the ways our lives have become easier—less work has led to less activity. But think of the ways that modern innovations and technology can be used to increase our connection to others and *promote* activity. Whether it's using an Internet search to find a dance class, connect with friends through social media, or look at an online calendar for bingo night, you can use cutting-edge resources to keep busy.

CHALLENGE CHECKLIST

- [ ] Set up at least one social media account like Facebook or Instagram and link to family or friends.

- [ ] Plan an online game such as Risk or chess with a friends or family who live too far away for a face-to-face game.

☐ Send a group email to friends or family with updates on your life, and be sure to attach photos.

☐ Download solitaire or a word game to your phone or tablet.

☐ Subscribe to a special-interest blog or newsletter.

☐ Use technology to find at least one social event to attend every month.

☐ Add a helpful app to your smartphone or tablet, like a level, a flashlight, or a compass.

☐ Watch drone footage of your favorite exotic destination using an online video service. Options include YouTube, Vimeo, Twitch, Dailymotion, Metacafe, Photobucket, Flickr, and Veoh.

☐ Use an online service to find your next vacation destination.

☐ Try booking your next doctor's appointment using his or her website.

☐ Search YouTube to find a new exercise routine.

☐ Use a fitness watch or app to track steps.

3

Walk on the
Wild Side

challenge your comfort zone

"Do not be too timid and squeamish about your actions.
All life is an experiment.
The more experiments you make, the better."
—Ralph Waldo Emerson, American author and philosopher

When was the last time you did something outside your comfort zone or broke your routine?
When we stay in our comfort zone, we're surrounded by
the familiar and feel safe and secure. That's a wonderful
thing because our comfort zone is peaceful and relatively
stress-free, but it's also limiting. So it's important to
shake things up from time to time. Don't panic—I'm not

suggesting anything as wild as cliff diving or downhill skateboarding. The idea is to do something that's just wild enough to invigorate our spirit and refresh our energy.

Being able to put aside our preconceived ideas and view things from a different perspective helps us grow in life. Oliver Wendell Holmes said, "One's mind, once stretched by a new idea, never regains its original dimensions." Pursuing activities outside our comfort zone can truly change how we think and help us learn more about the people and the world around us.

I'm a huge fan of romantic comedies, so when I think of the topic of comfort zones, the 1987 movie *Overboard* springs to mind. The lighthearted story is about a self-absorbed socialite (Goldie Hawn) who's condescending to those around her, including an impoverished contractor (Kurt Russell) she refuses to pay for a project. When she loses her memory, he convinces her that she's his wife and the mother of his four children. By the time she regains her memory, she has adapted to a life of hard work, learned to compromise, and become empathetic.

After she returns to her opulent lifestyle, she feels guilty about her past behavior.

In an honest moment with her long-suffering butler, she confides that everyone thinks she's crazy and wonders if he has the same opinion. His response to her is one of those scraps of movie dialogue that have always stayed with me. "Oh no, madam. Oh no," he says. "... most of us go through life with blinders on, madam. Knowing only that one little station to which we were born. But now you, madam, on the other hand, had the ... rare privilege of escaping your bonds for just a spell. To see life from an entirely new perspective. How you choose to use that information, madam ... is entirely up to you."

It's a simple concept and one that can have significant impact on our understanding of others and our empathy for them. Give yourself the opportunity to see things from an entirely new perspective. Try an activity that's out-of-character, especially if it's something you've always secretly wanted to do. If you want to go to a water park, go even if you're self-conscious about wearing a bathing suit.

Think about ways you could complete this sentence: "I'm not the kind of person who ..." Are you not the kind of person who goes to a movie or restaurant alone? Spearheads a community project? Enters baking contests? Goes on vacation at a dude ranch?

If not, why not? Don't hold back—break out of the rut and do it anyway. Our attitudes and outlook on life are usually based on the experiences that have shaped our beliefs. Challenging those beliefs and trying something we might consider a little wild can open up a new world of understanding and allow for personal growth.

Add to Your Experience
new experiences lead to new understanding

"Nothing ever becomes real
till it is experienced."
—John Keats, English poet

Throughout our lives, we learn through experience, adding knowledge and personal opinions to our understanding of the world—what we like, what we fear, what tastes good, what things are beautiful. At any point, who we are as a person and how we think is based on the sum total of our experiences. As long as we're alive, we can keep adding to that total. We can have new experiences that affect our understanding and attitudes. It stands to reason that the more diverse the experiences are, the greater the sum total of our life. And we'll never know how much we're truly capable of until we step out of our comfort zone.

When I was forty-six, I saw a flier for the Warrior Dash —a 5K course with twelve obstacles scattered over rugged terrain—and casually mentioned to a girlfriend that I wished I were the type of person who could do something like that. "If you think it sounds like fun, go for it," she said. "There's no reason not to."

I had no idea if I was capable of meeting the challenge, but she was so sure I could do it that I took a closer look at the event details. It was comforting to find out I could walk instead of run the entire five kilometers, but the obstacles included mud pits, rope swings, walls to be scaled, and even a fire trench. It seemed difficult, but the brochure promised it was appropriate for all fitness levels, from extreme athletes to couch potatoes.

I was excited and skeptical at the same time. I'd never been much of an athlete but always wished I possessed the fitness and stamina to participate in events like these. And it wasn't just the physical challenge that seemed daunting —I found the entire idea intimidating. The crowds, the possibility that participants who were more physically fit would judge me, and the prospect of being covered in mud were only a few of my concerns. But I'd said I wanted to do something completely out-of-character, so I registered for the Warrior Dash and committed to a fitness program to prepare.

Over the six weeks of training, I questioned my decision more than once. I'd worked a desk job for twenty-five years and was hardly a fitness buff. On the day of the race, I still wasn't sure if I was ready. It was Father's Day, the sun was shining, and the weather was a perfect seventy degrees.

As we lined up at the starting line, I felt my stomach clench, and I struggled to keep my feet planted. My nervousness made me jittery. I just hoped I wouldn't make a fool of myself.

But within five minutes of the start, something unexpected happened: I started to relax. Several things had quickly become apparent. First, no one was paying any attention to me. Second, when that the initial obstacle, a five-foot-deep mud pit, presented itself less than a half-mile into the course, endurance for long-distance running or jogging wasn't a factor. Finally, all the pull-ups and the hours on the stair-climber had been unnecessary. The obstacles weren't as challenging as I'd imagined. And I'm not sure that any exercise I could have done at the gym could have adequately prepared me for the specific challenge of jumping into a pit of mud and clawing my way up the opposite side. But that's just what I did.

The course was a dirt path about ten feet wide that started out in a grassy field and quickly entered a grove of trees. A section about four feet wide and five feet deep had been dug out in the middle of the path, and I joined the other participants as we jumped into the trench and trudged across, the water at the bottom lapping above my ankles. I felt my feet sink in the mud and it sucked at my shoes, making each step a battle. When I finally reached the other side, I had to climb up a dirt wall with no hand-holds, no foot-holds, and no tools. At five-foot-three, I could reach up and feel the ground above me, but I couldn't stretch enough to get a grasp and pull myself up. Jumping proved futile as well. With no other choice, I jammed my fingers into the dirt, thankful that my finger-nails were fairly long. And they did the job—I was able to dig into the gooey wall, creating just enough leverage to pull myself up as mud squished between my fingers.

I was glad the organizers had put the mud pit first because after encountering that slimy mess, my squeamishness vanished. I didn't hesitate to swim neck-deep through a fifty-foot channel or slither on the ground in an elbow crawl under barbed wire.

If someone has suggested to me a year before that I would not only enter such a race but that I would finish it, I wouldn't have believed I was capable of such a feat. But by the time I crossed the finish line, I'd slopped through several mud challenges, navigated a balance beam while being pelted with water spouts, and even jumped across a small pit of fire. I *was* capable of it.

The experience was exhilarating and more fun than I'd had in years. The course took less than ninety minutes to complete, and that's all it took to change my outlook on so many things. With that achievement under my belt, I felt like there was nothing I couldn't accomplish if I wanted it.

THE CHALLENGE
FIND YOUR WILD SIDE

"Great things never came from comfort zones."
—Anonymous

Stepping out of your comfort zone doesn't have to be a big jump. It can be something small. Every new experience helps us grow as a person by expanding our understanding and appreciation for life. Getting outside our comfort zones and deliberately taking on challenges on our own terms can help us deal with unexpected changes when they happen.

CHALLENGE CHECKLIST

☐ Go to a movie or out for dinner by yourself.

☐ Enter a contest—poetry-writing, baking, whatever.

☐ Attend a masquerade party in an unlikely costume.

☐ Toboggan down a ski slope.

☐ Join a challenge like three-legged race or juggling.

☐ Attend something you've always assumed you'd dislike, such as the ballet, an escape room, or an educational seminar.

☐ Travel to a foreign country.

☐ Go horseback-riding.

☐ Sign up for a 5K walk.

☐ Perform in front of a group of people.

☐ Wear something in a color you've always avoided.

4

Celebrate Family and Heritage

savings memories for the next generation

"There are only two lasting bequests
we can give our children.
One of these is roots, the other, wings."
—Hodding S. Carter, American journalist

For many families, shared history creates a cherished connection. We share memories, traditions, and common interests. Maybe you have an ongoing game of chess or scrabble, get together to watch a favorite sports team, or work on projects like fixing a car or baking for holidays. Some families have traditions that originated centuries ago.

Having a connection to the past provides us with a sense of belonging. Understanding shared heritage can bring us closer to extended family like cousins and great-uncles, and it also provides an avenue for finding unknown branches of the family that share a common ancestry. For many people, finding those connections to additional relatives has become a hobby. Legal documents, census records, and immigration forms have become more accessible thanks to online tools, making genealogy research easier. Genealogy website services provide software for family trees, DNA testing, resource tools, and even articles about genealogy research. Sites like Ancestry.com, Archives.com, and FamilySearch.org offer a variety of services for a monthly fee and limited access at no charge.

A study commissioned by Ancestory.com indicated that the stories of ancestors aren't always shared with younger generations. Many children don't know who their great-great-grandfather was or the story of how their grandparents first met. In a poll of two thousand Americans, 20 percent of the respondents couldn't name one of their eight great-grandparents. Yet in the same study, 84 percent said it was important to know about their heritage.

One of the most common reasons people search for relatives and ancestors is the quest for personal histories, which sometimes include famous and even infamous family members. We can find out where our ancestors came from, what language they spoke, the story of how and where they immigrated, even the role they played in their community's history.

Experts agree that knowing our family history helps create emotional well-being, develops personal identity, and gives us a sense that we're connected to something bigger than ourselves—a sense of belonging. Family history provides roots and stability. And you can have a role in preserving those roots. By documenting the family you know today—recording your own experiences and the stories you know from your parents, grandparents, aunts, uncles, and other relatives—you can share wisdom, insight, and entertainment with future generations.

Grandparents can share family stories in the grand oral tradition as storytime during a visit or turn them into bedtime stories. And, of course, keeping a written record of the stories is an activity that's well worthwhile. A memoir or family history book is a permanent way to record memories and personal stories of family members and create connection and continuity from generation to generation. You can incorporate stories about family members who have particular talents, interesting hobbies, and noteworthy experience or education. Maybe you have an uncle who can tell you how to make the perfect fishing lure or an aunt who can show you how to grow prize-winning tomatoes. And don't forget the recipes! Everyone needs the recipes for Grandma's special snickerdoodle cookies, Thanksgiving stuffing, and the mouthwatering chicken and biscuits that she makes better than anyone else.

If you don't enjoy writing, consider an innovative approach. Grandmas Project was spearheaded by Jonas Pariente for that purpose. The premise is simple: provide a platform to allow sharing of recipes and stories of grandmas around the world through short videos filmed by their grandchildren. Let's face it—many grandmas cook by taste or touch, so recording a video of the process might be easier than getting a written copy. And many of today's grandchildren are experienced with social media and proficient in video recording, so they can record their grandmothers in their own kitchens as they make their favorite recipes and engage in casual conversation. The approach encourages storytelling and gives grandparents an opportunity to share the recipes' origins, family traditions, and childhood memories about the dishes they're preparing. Once the videos are uploaded, the website makes them available for public viewing along with the recipes.

If making a live video that will be seen publicly on the Internet doesn't appeal to you, consider using a similar approach to make a private historical record. You can create short videos of recipes for your family so your daughter-in-law or grandchildren will know how to properly re-create your signature dishes—and so will their children and grandchildren.

Think about your hobbies or skills you might like to teach family members. How about a video series from Grandpa about woodworking or car repair? You can also record yourself reading a series of short bedtime stories or chapters of classics like Swiss Family Robinson.

Whether you record something personal or share a favorite story, preserving history and memories is important to future generations. We can all benefit by knowing where we come from and learning about our ancestors.

According to Ancestry.com, one-third of adults who have Internet access used it to learn about their family history. Of them:

- 67 percent said that knowing their family history has made them feel wiser as a person.

- 72 percent said it helped them to be closer to older relatives.

- 52 percent said they discovered ancestors they had not known about.

It can take hours every week researching and creating family trees, logging the stories you come across, and making notes for more follow-up. But how do you begin a search? An easy, free place to start is the National Archives' Resources for Genealogists (https://www.archives.gov/research/genealogy). From the site, you can access old land records, census and military documents, immigration records such as ship manifests, and naturalization records. If the process sounds daunting, don't worry—the National Archives site has informative instructional videos on multiple topics that are easy to understand and follow.

Research into family genealogy can take as much or as little time as you want to invest. The first step is often the Internet, and while doing online research from home is convenient, the library can provide a more social setting, and librarians can answer questions if you need help. If your family has been in the same area for generations, you may find some record of them in old books or newspapers at your library.

Once you find an intriguing story or two—or an infamous relative—other family members may want to join in and help on the project. See where the investigation takes you. Literally. Plan a day trip to see gravesites or visit towns where an ancestor had roots. Stop in at the local newspaper office and library, where you may find photocopies of old newspapers or even the papers themselves that you can review. It's fun to find ancestors and read about them in old news stories.

If historical research doesn't appeal to you, you can embrace your heritage with a more direct approach. Local heritage groups exist to keep cultural traditions alive, and they can help you to keep those traditions alive in your own family. There are many clubs and organizations throughout the United States that connect people with their ancestry and cultural heritage. They hold social gatherings and meetings focused on preservation of the culture. You can join and learn about important traditions and how to incorporate them into your own family celebrations.

Embracing Ancestors
connecting with generations past

"Our heritage and ideals, our code and standards—
the things we live by and teach our children—
are preserved or diminished by how freely we
exchange ideas and feelings."
—Walt Disney, American film producer and businessman

Understanding our cultural heritage helps us to understand ourselves better and to feel connected to something larger. Family, extended family, culture, and heritage all contribute to who we are. For as long as I can remember, I've known that my mother was from Iceland, but during my childhood, it didn't have much impact on me other than being an interesting anecdote. I didn't understand the significance or importance of that heritage until I became an adult.

Mom had a strong desire to record and document her childhood memories to share with family and interested friends, so she wrote a memoir that included stories that occurred from the time she was ten to the time she was eighteen. As I read the published book, *Growing Up*

Viking: Fond Memories of Iceland, I was surprised that there were some stories I'd never heard before and other stories that included far greater detail than I'd ever known. I gained a greater understanding of my mom by reading it and developed a stronger connection with my ancestry. While I had always been proud of my Icelandic heritage and treasured that culture, reading her memories added a personal connection. The land and culture become more vibrant and real to me.

After Mom moved to the United States in 1945, when she'd tell someone she was from Iceland, they'd respond with a blank stare or a glazed-eye look. Not many people knew much about Iceland, which is understandable since even today its population is only about 350,000 and only about 50,000 people of Icelandic descent live in the United States. That's about half the population of the state of Wyoming.

Mom made it her mission to ensure that Iceland was recognized and had its fair representation. It was one reason she loved to participate in Scandinavian festivals and events. She relished the opportunity to talk about

Iceland and answer almost any question someone might ask. Once when she and one of my sisters were in an airport, they walked along a corridor decorated with hanging flags from various countries. There were so many that it seemed that every country in the world must be represented. Eagerly, Mom looked for Iceland's, but as they walked along, she started to lose hope. All the rest of the Nordic countries were there—Denmark, Norway, Sweden, Finland—but no Iceland.

"How could Iceland be ignored or forgotten?" she huffed. Her annoyance grew as she pointed out flags from countries even less populated than Iceland. "That one," she said, jabbing her finger in the air. "Hatu. They don't have a flag for Iceland, but they have Hatu. Who ever heard of Hatu?" After walking under the flag, she looked back, still exasperated. Suddenly she stopped and laughed, realizing they'd been looking at the back of the flag. "Oh, Utah. Not Hatu. I guess that's okay." And then she spotted it: the Icelandic flag. "Woo-hoo!" she shouted, happy that she wasn't going to have to kick up a fuss with airport management after all.

As an adult, I share that pride in my heritage and have learned about my ancestors through family members and online resources. The Íslendingabók, or Book of Icelanders, provides online records for nearly half the country's population. It also allows access to all available information on Icelanders born before 1700, but the entire database is in Icelandic, making research difficult for those who don't speak the language. Fortunately, there's also a resource that's mostly in English: the U.S.-based database Icelandic Roots, which was created for immigrants and descendants born in other parts of the world and also lists generations born in Iceland as early as 900 A.D. Many nationalities and heritage groups have such databases and similar resources available.

I've spent hours combing through the histories of my ancestors and have found kings, chieftains, and even a few famous Vikings. It was interesting to find out that I'm the twenty-nine-times great-granddaughter of King Harald I the Fair-Haired, the first king of Norway, and a thirty-one-times great-granddaughter of the legendary

Ragnar Lodbrok, well-known from the television show Vikings. (The Icelandic language has several unique letters that don't appear in other languages. The actual name is Loðbrók. The letter Eth "ð" is often translated to English as "d" but is pronounced with a "th-" sound.)

Cultural pride and heritage can bring families together. The process of research, documenting, recording, and sharing that heritage is a gift that we can give to future generations. Plus, it's just plain fun.

THE CHALLENGE
CONNECT WITH YOUR HERITAGE

"Preserve your memories, keep them well,
what you forget you can never retell."
—Louisa May Alcott, American poet and author

When we think about family and heritage, we often lump them together as a general topic, but it really is made up of two parts: future and past. The traditions and memories saved for future generations and the research it takes to uncover the forgotten past. What can you do that will connect your knowledge to future generations? What can you embrace from the past?

CHALLENGE CHECKLIST

☐ Write down your favorite recipes and some from your parents and grandparents, if you can, to share with the next generation.

☐ Share the stories of traditions from your family history with the youngest generation.

☐ Record a video of yourself reading your favorite book or poem.

☐ Make a family-related craft.

☐ Join a genealogy group to create a family tree or add to the information you already have.

☐ Choose an ancestor to research.

☐ Join a local heritage organization to learn more about your family's cultural history, or several if you've discovered ancestors from several countries.

☐ Try new foods or recipes that come from your ancestors' homelands.

☐ Add a heritage tradition to your celebrations.

☐ Find and attend a heritage festival.

5

Take the Scenic Route

finding more than nature

"If you are not willing to risk the unusual,
you will have to settle for the ordinary."
—Jim Rohn, American author

Taking the scenic route usually means taking the long way or even dawdling instead of traveling in an efficient, timely manner. Although it's a cliché, taking the scenic route is an opportunity to slow down, relax, and savor the trip. It's about the journey, not the destination, right?

Unfortunately, that's rarely the case anymore. Today if you need to drive somewhere that's any distance away, you're likely to take the interstate. It's fast and easy, with frequent exits conveniently marked with food, fuel, and overnight accommodations. It's a system designed to facilitate travel from Point A to Point B as quickly as possible. But the downside of interstate travel is that it can be monotonous and boring. There's little opportunity for exploration or adventure. The fastest isn't always the best, and it's rarely the most interesting.

In Wyoming, if you need to go from Interstate 80 at Rawlins to Interstate 25 at Casper, you have to use the smaller state highways. The 116-mile stretch takes about an hour and a half to drive unless you decide to take in every bit of scenery along the way, in which case it takes seven hours. I happen to know this because that's exactly what Mom and I did on our drive between Utah and South Dakota one year. My plan had been an efficient fifteen-hour route, but when we came across the opportunity to explore, neither of us could resist. Mom had instilled her sense of curiosity in me by setting the example while I was growing up. She always wondered about the world. What's over the hill? What do you think that tower over there is? How things were made, the history of a place, and a famous person's story were all topics of discussion at our house. So when we saw the sign for the Mormon Handcart Museum, I didn't hesitate to stop.

As it turned out, the museum was filled with artifacts and personal belongings from the people who had made the thirteen hundred-mile trek from Illinois to Utah *on foot* from 1846 to 1868. We spent over an hour in the small building, looking at the exhibits and reading the stories, captivated by the travelers' tenacious spirit and determination. It was inspiring and humbling to see that even though they had few possessions, they had the stamina and strength to stay the course and complete the journey.

The curator told us that Martin's Cove, a site where a group of Mormon emigrants sheltered during a winter storm, was only two miles down the road, so we decided to check that out, too. I drove while Mom studied the brochure and found a map of walking trails. We easily found the trailhead for a one-mile hike to Devil's Gate, a gorge on the Sweetwater River that the brochure said was a major landmark on the emigrants' journey. The "gate" is only thirty feet wide at the bottom, but at the top it's almost three hundred feet—the length of a football field. The strip of land between the river and the massive rock formations wasn't wide enough for emigrants to pass through with their belongings, but many of them stopped to carve their names in the rocks or to buy supplies at the trading post.

The trail was well-worn, and we read on the signs that the path had been used for annual reenactments of the pushcart immigration. It was nearly wide enough to be called a road, and the surface was hard-packed to the point that it felt like pavement. It was an easy walk, and we were enjoying the time in the sunshine of the seventy-degree day. The trail seemed to dead-end at a small creek that flowed from between large rock formations to our left. It was as if a giant ax had cut a sliver out of a massive rock wall. We stood for a moment, admiring the view, and our momentary silence allowed us to catch the distant sound of rushing water. We exchanged a look, but no words were necessary. It sounded like a waterfall, and that was one of Mom's favorite sights. If there was a waterfall nearby, we wanted to find it.

We followed the sound, scrambling over a few boulders that were easy to climb, worn away as if they'd been smoothed by hundreds of explorers before us. We eventually came to a rock that was well over six feet high and seemed to be the base of the Devil's Gate. The cliffs towered over us on either side, and directly in front of us was a large boulder with a set of wooden steps propped against one side, obviously placed there to aid hikers. We climbed to the top of the boulder and followed the sound of the crashing water down a narrow path between the two cliffs, which angled higher as we walked.

We never did find the waterfall, but when we turned around to head back, the view was breathtaking, and that alone was worth the trip. We could see a valley below, the creek winding its way around until it disappeared in the distance. Aside from the trail, the visitor center, and the small parking lot, there were empty plains as far as the eye could see. It was May and apparently too early for tourists—we had the place to ourselves. It was easy to imagine what the emigrants saw when they traveled through Devil's Gate: a land populated by bighorn sheep and antelope, and what seemed to be miles of knee-high green grasses rippling in the breeze—a lot like what we were looking at.

After making our way back to the loop trail that led to the parking lot, we headed down the road again. But less than thirty minutes later, I saw Independence Rock on the horizon, and as an avid reader of historical fiction, I couldn't pass up the opportunity to touch the famed rock. I'd read many accounts of wagon trains headed west and the wagon masters determined to reach Independence Rock by the Fourth of July because if they didn't, they would probably be trapped in the mountain passes by snow. As they traveled across the plains, they could see the rock for miles before they reached it, no surprise considering that it's 136 feet high, 700 feet wide, and almost 2,000 feet long. When the wagon trains made it to this landmark along the Sweetwater River, they'd stop to rest and celebrate. It was a rite of passage for the travelers to carve initials and messages into the rock face, and it was an unexpected pleasure to touch the rock that so many hands had touched before mine.

As fascinating as those 116 miles are, I'm surprised it's not officially designated a scenic route by the Federal Highway Administration. The designation is given to America's most outstanding roads as part of the National Scenic Byways Program, which promotes and helps preserve them through special funding. The only way to get the designation is for the local community to request it through the state. The routes have to have at least one of six specific qualities: scenic, natural, historic, recreational, archaeological, or cultural. Communities benefit not only from the preservation and improvement of the road but also from the marketing, which translates to visitors and helps local economies.

You can find a full list of the Scenic Byways on the Department of Transportation's website (https://www. fhwa.dot.gov/byways/). Since there are a hundred and fifty throughout the United States, opportunities for adventure are nearly endless.

Curiosity Is the Cure for Boredom
cultivate your curiosity

"When you're curious,
you find lots of interesting things to do."
—Walt Disney, American film producer and businessman

Taking the scenic route is the perfect way to indulge—or cultivate—your sense of curiosity. Did you know that curiosity has health benefits? Being curious has been linked with positive emotions, a sense of well-being, and reduced stress. It might be the anticipation of a new experience, the excitement of adventure, or the simple satisfaction of accomplishment that we have when we conquer something new. Whatever the reason, the science shows that curiosity is good for us.

Whether it's taking the longer route to the grocery store or adding some off-the-interstate sections to your next trip, it's fun to indulge in exploration. Of course, there are some other benefits as well.

Less Traffic

Once you leave the interstate behind, you can expect less traffic. The scenic route usually has fewer vehicles, but you don't have to actually drive at all. Buses and trains are cost-effective options that allow you to fully enjoy the scenic route.

Riding trains has the extra advantage of offering views of scenic landscapes we could never even glimpse from the highway. Amtrak, for instance, has routes such as The Adirondack from New York to Montreal, which criss-crosses the wine country of the Hudson Valley. The Amtrak California Zephyr route runs between Denver and San Francisco and has been called one of the most beautiful train trips in North America. It takes you through the heart of the Rockies, Ruby Canyon, the red rocks of Utah, Donner Pass in the Sierra Nevada, and right up to the Pacific Ocean.

Bus trips, on the other hand, can be designed around destinations, events, or activities. Like with trains, you can select a specific area to visit, but you can also choose a location and an event. How about a tour of California wineries? Or New England in the autumn as the colors are in their full splendor? Maybe something even more relaxing? Like one of the many paddlewheel riverboats operating on the Mississippi and other rivers throughout the United States? Floating down the middle of a river gives us a completely different view.

The Scenery

The Interstate Highway System was designed for high-speed, high-capacity travel. Some of the roads offer scenic overlooks, but to see many of the best sites we have to get off the interstate. As an example, Peoria, Illinois, is well-known for its beautiful river views, but you can't see them from the interstate. One of the local television stations is even named WMBD, call letters that stand for "World's Most Beautiful Drive." Local legend attributes the statement to President Theodore Roosevelt in describing Peoria's two-and-a-half-mile Grandview Drive that runs along the hillside overlooking the Illinois River. The waterway is a broad blue-green swath, and trees are thick on the opposite shore, providing an array of colors in the fall.

Whether it's the Grand Canyon in Arizona, Arches National Park in Utah, Yellowstone in Wyoming and Montana, Sequoia and Kings Canyon National Park in California, the Angel Oak Tree in Charleston South Carolina, Mount Rushmore in South Dakota, or the Hill Country of Texas, some of America's best scenery can't be seen from the interstate.

Quirky & Unusual Attractions

Taking a trip off the beaten path can lead to some unusual man-made attractions. All across America, there are unique destinations you might not soon forget.

In Alliance, Nebraska, you can see a replica of Stonehenge created from vintage American automobiles, painted the same shade of gray as the famous site in England. Just outside Dothan, Alabama, there's a giant metal hog—

thirteen feet tall and twenty-six feet long—standing in a scrap metal yard. And North Dakota's Enchanted Highway provides views of an entire collection of metal artwork, specifically prairie animals.

In Dyersville, Iowa, you can visit the Field of Dreams— the baseball diamond in the middle of cornfields. It's a real place, and sometimes they even put up a big screen where you can watch a movie after dark. Whether you're a movie buff or a baseball fan, it's a spot on the scenic route that's worth a stop.

Historical Sights & Natural Wonders

The United States National Historic Landmark Program has more than twenty-five hundred designated landmarks that include structures, sites, and objects. Devil's Tower in Wyoming was the first site to be named a national monument, by President Theodore Roosevelt in 1906. It's the location featured in *Close Encounters of the Third Kind* and had been shrouded in supernatural mystery long before its movie fame. Legends about the site exist among many of the indigenous peoples in the area, but my personal favorite is from the Crow tribe.

In the Crow legend, the rock tower is called "Bear's House." As the story goes, one day, a hungry bear came upon two young girls playing near a large boulder. Terrified, the girls scrambled to the top of the rock. When the bear started up after them, the Great Spirit pushed the rock up, making it rise. The bear jumped up, trying to reach the girls, but its claws only caught on the rock, slashing deep ruts into the sides that are still visible to this day. The rock kept growing until it was so high the bear couldn't jump to the top, and the girls were safe.

Every state in America has beautiful scenery, and you can usually rely on the recommendation of a local to point you to the best spots. Chestnut Ridge Park in upstate New York has a flame that burns perpetually behind a waterfall, fed by a stream of natural gas. There's a spot off the coast in Cape Perpetua, Oregon, known as Thor's Well that looks like a bottomless sinkhole in the ocean, but it's only about twenty feet deep and definitely a sight to see.

Local Flavor & Food

When you walk into a national chain restaurant, you can count on consistent quality and rely on the familiarity of menu, decor, and service. When you stop at a locally owned restaurant, the unknown is part of the adventure. Many small-town eateries offer specialty dishes that you won't find anywhere else. You might find the juiciest steak, the best barbeque, and the most outstanding desserts at restaurants you've never even heard of. And everywhere we go, there are local flavors and special ways of preparing dishes that have their own appeal. For example, in South Dakota, the meat dish known as chislic is a common appetizer, but few people outside the state have heard of it. Similarly, crawfish is common along the Gulf Coast, but it's rare in other parts of the country. And when we're in an area with an Amish population, I'm always on the lookout for the delicious apple butter and jellies the Amish make. Wherever you travel, take time to enjoy the flavors and specialties!

Regional Shopping

Shopping can be a fun part of any trip, and once you leave the tourist centers behind, you can find shops that carry works from local artisans, handcrafted items, and other items with locally inspired motifs. Shops in Arizona and New Mexico have Southwestern flair that is distinctly different from the cowboy-inspired offerings of Texas and Oklahoma. Florida shops usually feature souvenirs with a casual beach motif, whereas many stores in the Northeast feature artists' works that have nautical themes.

For shopping enthusiasts, you can plan the destination around the type of shopping you enjoy. Bloomington, Minnesota, is home to Mall of America, the largest mall in the United States, with five hundred stores, ten attractions, and even an indoor theme park. If you want something farther south, the largest outlet mall in America is Sawgrass Mills, in Sunrise, Florida, outside Fort Lauderdale. And dedicated bargain-hunters will want to check out the 127 Yard Sale. For nearly seven hundred miles along Highway 127, you can shop yard sales through six states.

Starting in Michigan, the event continues through Ohio, Kentucky, Tennessee, Georgia, and Alabama. Mark your calendar—it's the first weekend of August every year.

THE CHALLENGE
EXPLORE
OFF THE BEATEN PATH

"Live for the moments you can't put into words."
—Kid Rock, American singer-songwriter

Going off the beaten path doesn't have to mean heading for a quiet or unexciting destination. In fact, it doesn't have to be a trip at all. Taking the long way or using an unfamiliar route can shake up your routine. Just look for opportunities to explore, and be open to the quirky and unexpected things you may find along the way.

CHALLENGE CHECKLIST

☐ Take a Sunday drive on a country road you've never traveled before.

☐ Plan a getaway using AARP resources like bus trips.

☐ Choose a drive in the Scenic Byways Program.

☐ Visit a nearby local or national park for a picnic.

☐ Take a train ride on one of Amtrak's scenic routes.

☐ Use AAA driving trips to plan a route.

☐ Spend a weekend antiquing or browsing secondhand shops in small towns.

☐ Pick a destination at least an hour away and plan a route that doesn't involve any interstates.

☐ Plan a weekend in the mountains or at a lake at least an hour away from a big town.

☐ Pick a few destinations from a list of wacky or unusual tourist stops.

☐ Spend an afternoon exploring a small town you've never visited.

6
Keep Learning
keep your mind young

> "It is not knowledge, but the act of learning,
> not possession but the act of getting there,
> which grants the greatest enjoyment."
> —Carl Friedrich Gauss, German mathematician and physicist

Have you ever wanted to play the guitar? Learn a foreign language? Maybe learn how to golf? If you've been putting off learning something new because you think you need a good reason to pursue it, here's one: learning actually helps to slow your brain's aging. Studies have shown that the process of learning is mentally stimulating and that this improves memory, preserves problem-solving ability, and even lowers the risk of Alzheimer's and delays the onset of dementia. The best news is that any type of learning is beneficial.

Learn Something Fun

Learning a new card game or dance can be a fun way to keep your mind active and sharp. Learning how to play a musical instrument offers all sorts of benefits for your brain and your emotional well-being along with opportunities to get together to play with others. Even for seniors with arthritis or limited mobility, music is an adaptable hobby. Once you start looking around, you may be surprised at the variety of classes and learning opportunities being offered nearby.

Many libraries, museums, community centers, and nature preserves offer classes and presentations on a wide range of topics. You can find classes about panning for gold, scrapbooking, and even how to use email. Classes like these are often free and usually only an hour or two, so you can try something without making a long-term commitment. And some colleges offer free courses for senior citizens (https://www.thepennyhoarder.com/save-money/free-college-courses-for-senior-citizens/).

One of the best resources for finding special-interest workshops is your local community college. The program might be called Lifelong Learning, Continuing Education, or Adult Community Programs, but they all have the same goals. Most lifelong learning programs offer non-credit courses, workshops, and seminars in a range of areas such as arts, fitness, computers, dance, photography, and even car maintenance and gardening.

Illinois Central College in East Peoria has offered estate planning seminars and classes in gun safety, meditation, garden pruning, upholstery, and cooking. I found out about these programs when my mom joined the staff to teach a six-week seminar called Decorating with Sheets. She was an interior decorator with a degree from the Institute of Design in Chicago and an expert seamstress, and every week she taught no-sew and little-sew projects for curtains, tablecloths, and home decorating, all using only bedsheets.

Continuing education can be enjoyable and personally enriching. Committing to a class or a program that's longer than a single class or two can have a more lasting impact, but whether you sign up for an hour class or a six-month course, you'll get the mental benefits of learning and probably social benefits, too.

Learn a Skill

Did you know that some abilities like expanding our vocabulary can actually improve with age? That's good news if you've always wanted to learn a foreign language. New technology and ease of travel have created a world-wide community. Many families have one or two members who live or have lived in foreign countries, and some have grandchildren who don't speak the same language. Whether that's the case for you or not, this might be the perfect time to start learning a new language. Since older adults have larger vocabularies, our brains can more easily associate words we know with the equivalents in a foreign language. Whether you want to learn one entire language or a few key phrases in many languages, you're never too old to start.

The benefit of having stronger vocabulary skills as we age is also good news if you'd like to take a writing class. When my mother retired, she finally had time to pursue a lifelong dream: writing a book. She signed up for a correspondence course and spent two years learning to write children's fiction. The fact that she was over eighty years old when she started didn't bother her a bit. Of course, learning another language and learning how to write well are just two examples of things we can learn at any age and continue to improve at and enjoy for years.

Hobbies like painting, woodworking, calligraphy, quilting, and cooking offer endless opportunities to learn the basics in a short period of time. And they also provide us with the opportunity for continual improvement. Whether you dabble in a lot of different things or devote yourself to reaching expert level in one pursuit, learning will help to keep your brain younger and healthier.

Learn for a New Career

Starting on a path of learning can even lead to a new career. Age is just a number, and it doesn't have to limit your education or career goals. There are lots of examples of older adults learning new skills or honing existing talents into substantial accomplishments. Julia Child worked in advertising before writing her first cookbook at the age of fifty. Laura Ingalls Wilder published her first book when she was sixty-five years old, what would turn out to be the start of the internationally popular *Little House on the Prairie* series. Anna Mary Robertson Moses—Grandma Moses—started painting when she was seventy-eight and created more than fifteen hundred works of art before she died at the age of one hundred and one.

Don't let the fear of being the oldest student in the room keep you from pursuing education. Time will pass either way, so ask yourself: do you want to be two years older and possess the knowledge you desire or be two years older and still wishing you'd taken the time to learn it?

Learning Has No Age Limit

"Anyone who stops learning is old,
whether at twenty or eighty.
Anyone who keeps learning stays young.
The greatest thing in life
is to keep your mind young."
—Henry Ford, American industrialist and businessman

More and more people over the age of fifty are taking on the challenge of a career change and even going back to college when they have college-age grandchildren themselves. Nearly 15 percent of students enrolled in community or four-year colleges are over the age of thirty-five, according to the National Center for Education Statistics. In Coursera, an online education platform offering thousands of free courses, 10 percent of the students are over the age of sixty.

Even if you're not looking to pursue a new career, taking college courses can be stimulating and enjoyable. Choose the topics that interest you the most, and you're sure to be pleased with the results. In addition to the mental benefits, you'll have the opportunity to expand your social group and increase your physical activity by going to classes on campus.

Many colleges and universities in the United States offer reduced or free tuition to senior citizens, but the rules and limitations vary by institution and state. The admissions department of your local college or university can provide details about specific programs.

When we learn, no matter what the topic or pursuit may be, we stimulate our mind and keep it sharp. When we apply what we've learned, we enhance our own lives and the lives of others.

THE CHALLENGE
HAVE FUN
LEARNING SOMETHING NEW

"What we learn with pleasure we never forget."
—Alfred Mercier, American physician

It's easy to think you're too old to learn something new. But not only is it possible, it's also good for you. What skills or ability have you always wanted to learn? What areas interest you? If you're not sure, challenge yourself and commit to one class. There's no such thing as wasted time if you're learning.

CHALLENGE CHECKLIST

☐ Sign up for a workshop at your local community college.

☐ Take an online class.

☐ Attend a paint-and-wine event.

☐ Sign up for a seminar or an hourlong class at the local library.

- [ ] Take a semester course at the local college.

- [ ] Read the biography of a famous person in history.

- [ ] Learn to play a musical instrument.

- [ ] Learn a foreign language or a few words in several languages.

- [ ] Take on a knitting, crocheting, or sewing project.

- [ ] Partner with a friend or a grandchild to learn about a topic they choose.

- [ ] Learn a new card game.

- [ ] Once a week, ask a question and then do research to learn about the topic:

  - [ ] How can I grow blueberries in my area?
  - [ ] What's the best way to photograph the moon?
  - [ ] What is chair yoga?
  - [ ] How do I refinish furniture?

7
Taste Life
food as an experience

"Laughter is brightest in the place where the food is."
—Irish proverb

We all know that food provides us with nutrition that fuels our bodies and keeps us healthy. We also know it's important to get the recommended amounts of nutrients and limit the indulgences that aren't good for us so that we can maintain a healthy heart, a strong immune system, and good overall health. But recent studies indicate that what we eat can also affect our moods and mental health.

In 2015, a study published in *Harvard Health,* a publication of Harvard Medical School, showed that while the digestive system's primary function is to process food, the gastrointestinal tract produces almost all the serotonin in our body. Serotonin has a critical function in regulating sleep and controlling appetite, but it also plays a role in maintaining healthy moods and inhibiting pain.

Staying physically healthy, sleeping well, and keeping balanced moods are all good reasons to strive for a healthy diet. But balanced nutrition—antioxidants and B vitamins are especially important—might also help to preserve brain function. Studies from Harvard's Brigham and Women's Hospital, Johns Hopkins University, and UCLA have shown that certain "brain foods" may slow the loss of cognitive function and memory and might even improve memory. Brain foods include green vegetables, fatty fish, berries, and walnuts.

But as we age, our sensitivity for both taste and smell diminishes, and our favorite foods can become less appealing. That can lead to eating less and not getting the nutrition we need, so it's important to find the balance between nutritional benefit and enjoyment. And that's why food is a perfect excuse for exploration and adventure, no matter where you live or what you typically eat.

When she was growing up in Iceland, my Mom's diet consisted primarily of fish, eggs, and dairy. Much of the native soil is volcanic and few crops grow there, so vegetables were mostly limited to rutabagas, potatoes, carrots, beets, and cabbage. They had a few green leafy vegetables, but Mom never acquired a taste for them. Even after more than twenty-five years in America, she called most vegetables "rabbit food" and rarely served them. As a result, I didn't develop a taste for vegetables either.

Healthy Doesn't Equal Boring

Whether our doctor tells us we need to change our diet or we decide to make the change ourselves, it can feel like a punishment. Of course, we don't want to give up the foods we love, and fortunately there are many ways to incorporate smaller amounts of our less healthy favorites into our diets. If there are foods that you have to give up completely, finding tasty replacements can be a fun treasure hunt. When we remove an item from our diet, it creates an opportunity to replace it with something new that we might like as much or even more. This is how Mom approached her doctor's advice after she had her stroke in 2016. She was ninety-one at the time, and she set out to learn more about heart health, cholesterol, and hidden ingredients such as the high sodium content in most packaged foods. She committed to healthier eating habits, though she never did manage to enjoy certain vegetables like spinach and kale.

I took on the vegetable challenge with her, and we decided to approach her dietary changes as an adventure. The secret to successfully eating healthily is to find foods you actually like. If you hate spinach, you're not going to eat it just because it's one of the healthiest greens. Instead of forcing it down, see if you can find a vegetable you like that has similar health benefits. Or maybe you just need to find a way to make spinach tasty or disguise the flavor.

For years I thought I disliked all healthy vegetables, primarily because I'd tried and didn't like some of the most common ones, such as spinach, broccoli, and green beans. Over time, I let my guard down and started cautiously trying more vegetables, and while I still haven't gained an appreciation for many salad ingredients, I have come across a few vegetables I find tasty in their natural form, like asparagus and zucchini. Others, like radishes, I've discovered I only like when they're prepared in specific ways. To me, raw radishes have a bitter taste and an unpleasant crunchy texture, but when they're quartered, tossed with olive oil and garlic and baked, they taste more like a slightly spicy baked potato.

To make the exploration more fun, turn it into an event by inviting some friends or family members to join you. You can go to your favorite restaurant and try something new from the menu or visit a different restaurant for the first time. These outings don't have to be about nutritional intake or staving off hunger—well, not *just* about that. We can turn mealtime into *fun* time by feeding all our senses. Everything from the cuisine to the décor and atmosphere can be enjoyable. For instance, if you're looking for a delicious meal where the preparation and presentation are fun and interactive, you might try a fondue restaurant for an entertaining change of pace. Picture dipping bite-size veggies into an array of melted cheeses and dunking bite-size fruits and sweets in melted chocolate. Yummy, right?

To broaden your appreciation for spices, flavors, and sauces that you use in dishes you make at home, try restaurants that offer cuisines from other regions and countries. You might discover that you even like broccoli if it's prepared with a certain blend of spices or flavors. During the summer, weekly farmers markets are colorful destinations, both for the produce and for the atmosphere. Take a few hours and see what new vegetables you can find to experiment with. If there's not a farmers market available, browse the produce department of a local grocery store or ethnic market to find different items.

Once you've selected some veggies, the experimentation can begin. I try to taste a small bite of a new vegetable before I decide how to prepare it. To be honest, nine times out of ten I don't like it, but by experimenting with different types of preparation, I can usually make it palatable. And sometimes I come up with something that's downright delicious, like my signature cauliflower banana muffins (recipe below). These cooking experiments can be done on your own, but sharing your results with others can make the effort even more rewarding. Just be sure to write things down as you go. There's nothing worse than creating something tasty and having no idea how you did it.

You'll Never Know Unless You Try
be willing to experiment

"Life expectancy would grow by leaps and bounds
if green vegetables smelled as good as bacon."
—Doug Larson, columnist

To make experimenting fun, it helps to be willing to have some big fails and to have an enthusiastic taste-tester. When I began my quest—not to make veggies taste better but to hide them in dishes I already liked—Mom was one of my early taste-testers, and she was willing to try anything I set in front of her. I'd been reading about how good kale is for us but I hate kale, so I was trying to figure out what I could put it in that would make the taste completely disappear. I decided to try adding dry kale to my ooey-gooey brown sugar-and-cinnamon rolls. Surely the flavors and the icing would do the trick. Mom and I took a bite at the same time, and I couldn't even choke mine down. She took a few sips of coffee, swallowed, and said, "It's not that bad with coffee." Her upbeat, positive outlook served her well but didn't make her the best food critic.

After that experiment, I relied on the honest feedback of my husband. I was determined to figure out how to hide healthy ingredients, not to simply mask their flavor. Cheddar cheese sauce on broccoli had never made the greens tasty for me, but I found that if I diced the broccoli and added it to a spicier nacho cheese sauce, the flavor was completely disguised. I was able to take an existing dish I liked and add to the nutritional value. I was thrilled at the discovery and rushed to apply the idea to other vegetables.

After much research, I made a list of ten vegetables with the highest nutritional value and gave myself the challenge of finding ways to work them into my daily diet. I'd had some success with adapting and adjusting recipes but much less with creating new recipes, so I set out to find recipes that included these high-nutrition vegetables that I could adapt to camouflage the original flavor as much as possible.

After early success with cauliflower and zucchini, I got cocky and moved on to brussels sprouts. One evening I prepared three different recipes that incorporated them: a hash of apples, bacon, and sprouts; baked sprouts with spicy barbecue sauce and bacon; and roasted sprouts with shallots, bacon, and pecans in a white wine sauce. Each had its own flavor profile, and I was confident that I'd created three outstanding culinary delights.

I proudly served my husband the plate with a flourish, and as I placed my own on the table and sat down, the aroma was undeniably heavenly. The first bite told a different story, though. I gingerly nibbled on each dish, trying to will my taste buds to approve, but to no avail. I looked at Raymond, who's a big fan of vegetables in nearly any form, and he was working hard to control his expression.

"Well? What do you think?" I said, not sure I wanted to hear the answer.

"Honey," he replied, shaking his head, "I have to say, this is a terrible thing to do to bacon."

Although the first round with Brussels sprouts was a colossal failure, it's now a funny memory. And I did eventually find ways to incorporate nearly all ten of the healthy selections into tasty dishes. These days, I continue to enjoy the exploration, but now I only include one experiment with each tried-and-true meal.

One of my favorite and easiest "supercharged" nutritional recipes is cauliflower-banana muffins. Cauliflower is one of those vegetables that are a good source of nutrients, and it has a mild flavor that's easy to disguise. I start with a simple banana muffin recipe and add riced cauliflower, or cauliflower "flour." To make the flour, simply wash the cauliflower and break off the florets. Grind it in a food processor until it resembles rice, or grate it by hand to achieve the right consistency. Strain the flour with cheesecloth to remove any excess water. You can store it in the refrigerator for a few days until you're ready to use it.

Cauliflower-Banana Muffins

3 large ripe bananas, mashed
¾ cup sugar
½ cup riced cauliflower
1 teaspoon baking soda
1½ cups flour

⅓ cup melted butter
1 egg, slightly beaten
1 teaspoon baking powder
½ teaspoon salt

1. In a medium bowl, mash bananas with a spoon or pastry cutter. Stir in melted butter and mix until bananas are smooth.

2. Add sugar and egg and mix until combined. Add riced cauliflower.

3. In a separate bowl, mix flour, baking powder, baking soda, and salt. Stir to blend ingredients; then add to banana batter.

4. Fold to blend, but do not overmix.

5. Bake at 375 degrees for 20 minutes. Makes six large or twelve small muffins.

THE CHALLENGE
TASTE SOMETHING NEW

"Pull up a chair. Take a taste. Come join us.
Life is so endlessly delicious."
—Ruth Reichl, American chef and food writer

When it comes to food, we can fall into routines. Think about your favorite meals and the foods you eat most often. When was the last time you tried something new? Went to a new restaurant? Tested a new recipe? Are there any foods you've avoided simply because of the flavor or perhaps some you've never tried solely based on the looks or the smell? Challenge yourself to try something new.

CHALLENGE CHECKLIST

☐ Choose an unfamiliar cuisine and make a list of restaurants to try.

☐ Have a fondue night—at home or at a restaurant if there's one if your area.

☐ Make a list of the top veggies you don't like and then try different ways of preparing them.

☐ Go to a farmers market and pick a veggie you've never tried before.

☐ Go to a local food tasting event.

☐ Attend a cooking class—your local library might have one.

☐ Try something new from the menu at your favorite restaurant.

☐ Follow a cooking blog or social media group to get new recipe ideas.

☐ Plan a progressive dinner (safari supper) with friends or neighbors. You have only one item per house or location—appetizer, main dish, side dish, dessert.

☐ Go to the library and check out a cookbook (or buy one) for a specific cooking style or preparation, like Crock-Pot recipes, grilling, or cheesecakes. I've personally had a lot of fun with one called Stuffed, from Publications International.

8

Give Time

volunteering can open up
a whole new world

"As you grow older, you will discover
that you have two hands—one for helping yourself,
the other for helping others."
—Audrey Hepburn, British actress and humanitarian

Giving time as a volunteer doesn't have to be a tedious experience or solely altruistic. The needs are great and varied across many organizations, and it's easy to find ways to help others that are fulfilling and maybe even fun. Joining one or several service organizations can also expand your social group, giving you an opportunity to meet people who have the same social concerns and passions as you have.

After retirement, investing time to help others can be especially important. Without the challenge and sense of accomplishment gained from work, life can seem to lose some of its meaning, and volunteering helps bring some of that meaning back. It provides a way to give back to the community and experience a sense of self-accomplishment.

Mary Hidalgo of Sunnyvale, California, who celebrated her hundredth birthday in 2020, still gives one day a month to a local museum where she's been volunteering for thirty-eight years. She's also passionate about serving veterans and volunteered more than twenty thousand hours over sixteen years at VA hospitals, and she's still volunteering at the American Legion Auxiliary. When a *Mercury News* reporter asked her if she had advice for living a long and happy life, she said, "Keep busy, keep out of trouble, keep a sense of humor and enjoy life."

Being a volunteer doesn't mean you have to make a commitment to a regular daily or weekly schedule or even a fixed number of hours. There are many one-time needs you can help to fill, and some of them are a lot of fun. When I lived in Illinois, one of my favorite events was the Morton Pumpkin Festival. Not only am I a big fan of pumpkin, but I love small-town festivals of every kind, so when the Chamber of Commerce was looking for volunteers, I signed up. My assignment was working for one hour at the Sweet Shack booth, the primary location for all things pumpkin: ice cream, cheesecake, muffins, milkshakes, and cookies. It seemed that everyone who attended the festival came through that line, and having a few minutes to chat with each person as I provided the treats was a lot more fun than simply attending the festival.

If you have a lot of time on your hands, you can become a big part of something and make a real difference to an organization. If you only have a few hours to give or aren't even sure that volunteering is for you, there's still a need for you to fill. Find something you believe in or are passionate about.

Even if you don't think you have a talent or gift for helping others, your desire to help protect a historical site, preserve nature, or increase literacy is all you need. In Illinois, I joined a group that mixed socializing with nonprofit events and projects. The organizers worked with local nonprofit agencies to meet needs in the community. Whether it was making emergency packages at the food bank for disaster relief or helping to renovate the library at a local orphanage, each effort was appreciated by the organization. I participated as often as I could, as it was a pleasure to be a part of a team that made a difference. It felt good to help others, and I appreciated making new friends.

After I moved away from the area, I missed the interaction and found ways to contribute to my new communities. There are many organizations that need volunteers. If you've never done volunteer work, there are a few places in your community that are sure to welcome your help:

- Church
  - Help with an annual bazaar or carnival.

- Provide cookies/desserts for meetings or dinner for bereaved people.

- Sign up for nursery or children's church.

- Help with odd jobs, cleaning, or lawn care.

• Community or senior center

- Serve on the board or help out in the office.

- Read or play games with residents/attendees.

- Organize fundraisers.

• Hospitals and Veterans Administration

- Read aloud to patients.

- Work at the reception desk or gift shop.

- Help plan and perform special events and celebrations.

- Visit the VA website for more information: https://www.volunteer.va.gov/

• Library

- Assist with children's craft projects and story hours.

- Create bulletin board displays.

- Sort book donations.

- Help create newsletters and flyers.

- Animal shelters and rescue centers

  - Help with feedings and cleaning the facility.

  - Walk dogs.

  - Take photos of animals for adoption.

  - Foster a pet.

- Schools

  - Help with carnivals and fundraisers.

  - Become a tutor.

  - Volunteer to speak on career day or about a special-interest topic.

- Food pantries

  - Help assemble food boxes.

  - Distribute boxes.

  - Organize fundraising.

- Museums

  ○ Work at the reception/information desk.

  ○ Serve as a tour guide.

  ○ Play a character in historical reenactments.

If you have a specific interest area, national-level organizations can help you find volunteer opportunities. If you worked in an office before retiring, a number of organizations would welcome those skills. A website called VolunteerMatch.org makes it easy to find out about needs, based on topics and specific geographical areas. Nonprofit organizations post requests for help ranging from office support to graphic design to mentoring small-business owners and everything in between. When you start looking, you'll find substantial needs in a surprising variety of areas. You can find local connections through national organizations like VolunteerMatch.org or check with your volunteer connection center.

A Lifetime of Experience
put your knowledge to use
"The meaning of life is to find your gift.
The purpose of life is to give it away."
—William Shakespeare

The skills you've acquired throughout your lifetime are valuable no matter what your age. Years in the workforce have given you a wealth of knowledge and ability in specific areas that can benefit nonprofit organizations. The skills perfected from hobbies and leisure pursuits can also be used to help others. Repurposing your knowledge and abilities into volunteer work for causes you believe in can be deeply rewarding.

For instance, the talents required for growing a flower or vegetable garden at home can translate to taking care of the grounds at your church or starting a garden at a community center. Experience and skills acquired during years spent in the workforce or natural abilities in areas such as music or art can be applied to many volunteer opportunities.

Sharing your knowledge and wisdom with the youngest generations can be especially rewarding, not to mention mutually beneficial. Known as *intergenerational volunteering*, the idea is to enhance interaction between seniors and children. Seniors are able to share knowledge gained from a lifetime of experiences, passing on skills to the next generations, and in turn they learn about new technology and innovations from the youngsters. Besides the skills they learn, the children build positive attitudes about aging.

In Cleveland, the Reading Mentor Program at the Intergenerational Schools has more than seventy volunteers who work with children to improve reading skills and build relationships with them by sharing stories. The goal is to instill a passion for reading and create lifelong readers, not simply to provide instruction for basic reading skills.

You can volunteer directly with a local school or become involved with a program like AARP's Foundation Experience Corps. The AARP program connects volunteers with teachers and schools to help children become strong readers by the end of third grade.

For those who love the outdoors, the National Park Service needs volunteers to take photographs, lead tours, and work at information centers. Some of these part-time jobs involve strenuous outdoor work, while others are less demanding, such as volunteering at civil war reenactments. You never know what enjoyable activities you can find until you look.

The federal website https://www.volunteer.gov/ provides listings of all the volunteer positions available, and you can filter the search with a number of parameters. The postings give you all the information you need. Here's an example:

VISITOR CENTER ASSISTANT
Shiloh National Military Park

ADDRESS: 1055 Pittsburg Landing Road, Shiloh, TN 38376

CONTACT: Timothy Arnold, 731-689-5696

AVAILABILITY: 2/1/2016-12/31/2020

CREATED: 1/17/2020

SUITABILITY: adults, seniors

DIFICULTY: not difficult

Whatever you find interesting, have some talent for, or just want to try, you can probably find related volunteering opportunities. If you enjoy music, joining the church choir can be rewarding, and since it's a group, there's less performance pressure if you have some stage fright. And who doesn't like the idea of Christmas caroling? The joy a song brings to someone else can't help but make the singer feel good.

If you're musically gifted and enjoy sharing your talent, consider an organization like Musicians on Call (https://www.musiciansoncall.org/). Based on a belief in the healing power of music, this organization connects musicians and singers with hospitals and health care facilities throughout the United States. Volunteers perform live music in common areas for patients and their families and also play in patients' rooms.

If you don't have musical talent or you want something more challenging to sink your teeth into, there's an organization that can give you the opportunity to help solve real problems. If you haven't heard of the Federal Crowdsourcing and Citizen Science initiative, check it out. You can volunteer to help with projects that benefit your local area such as monitoring air quality or observing water levels and even help with global projects like analyzing images of kelp forests or trapping backyard beetles. The idea is to engage the American public with federal government and nongovernmental organizations to solve problems together. The Federal Crowdsourcing and Citizen Science Catalog has more than four hundred projects that need volunteers. To begin helping to solve complex problems in our society, browse the catalog at https://www.citizenscience.gov/catalog/#.

Other organizations like Habitat for Humanity help build or renovate homes for people in need. Habitat for Humanity also has a special program called RV Care-A-Vanners that allows retirees who spend weeks or months in RVs to volunteer at project sites that coincide with their travels.

Whether you have time on your hands and want to help, have a talent you want to share, or have a lifetime of skills you want to put to good use, there's an organization that will benefit from your participation.

THE CHALLENGE
FIND FUN
WHILE VOLUNTEERING

"Don't ever question the value of volunteers.
Noah's Ark was built by volunteers;
the Titanic was built by professionals."
—Unknown

You don't have to have any special skills or prior experience to volunteer. Your time is the most important element. If you're unsure, choose to volunteer once for an hour or two. Try out different organizations to find one that works for you. Challenge yourself to get involved in one or two nonprofit efforts to find one you enjoy.

CHALLENGE CHECKLIST

☐ Volunteer for a Scholastic book fair at a local school.

☐ Join a park or river cleanup crew.

☐ Read to children at the local library story hour.

☐ Volunteer to make cookies for a local blood drive.

☐ Volunteer at a museum or historical center.

☐ Join a letter-writing or card club for deployed military members.

☐ Donate a few hours to a local hospital or VA center.

☐ Contact your church for programs that need volunteers.

☐ Join a food drive effort.

☐ Contact the local chamber of commerce for special-events volunteering.

☐ Consider an AARP-sponsored program.

☐ Volunteer at a local animal shelter or nature center.

9

Be a Hometown Tourist

vacation without the travel

> "It's not necessary to go far and wide.
> I mean, you can really find exciting and
> inspiring things within your hometown."
> —Daryl Hannah, American actress and environmental activist

Daryl Hannah's hometown of Chicago is known for deep-dish pizza, the Magnificent Mile, and a skyline with four of the tallest buildings in America. When you're a tourist, you can find some of those gems in guidebooks or through other research before visiting. But what about your own town? What if you've missed some of its hidden treasures?

Just because you've lived somewhere for a long time doesn't mean you've been to or even know about all the things a tourist might come to see. To discover what you might have missed, become a hometown tourist and explore the history, events, attractions, and points of interest in your own backyard.

After I moved from Central Illinois to Lake Preston, South Dakota, I gained a new hometown. But I didn't find out about the historical significance of the area until, completely by chance, I read a placard outside a local grocery store in nearby De Smet. To my delight, the building had initially been the feed store where Almanzo Wilder worked. He was the husband of Laura Ingalls Wilder, whose *Little House on the Prairie* series I'd read as a young girl. The books told of one family's adventures on the American frontier in the last few decades of the 1800s. The Ingalls had moved from Wisconsin to Kansas and then Minnesota before finally settling in De Smet, South Dakota, which was the setting for the last five books of the series (*By the Shores of Silver Lake*, *The Long Winter*,

Little Town on the Prairie, These Happy Golden Years, and *The First Four Years*). Many of the landmarks mentioned in the books, such as the Ingalls family homestead, the schoolhouse, the surveyor's house, and even Silver Lake itself, are real and open for tourist visits.

I was tickled to be living near a place of such historical significance but quickly found that the appeal of the area went far beyond the Ingalls legacy. I discovered lakes for boating and fishing, parks, hiking trails, shops with locally made items, and a pleasant winery right down the road. My new hometown of Lake Preston also has a museum housed in an old church with collections of military uniforms and memorabilia, antique farming implements, kitchen and homemaking items, school photos, and copies of the local newspaper dating back almost to the town's founding in 1882.

While I was leaving the museum after my first visit, I spotted a brochure for "14 Museums on Highway 14." Intrigued, I picked it up and learned that the towns in the area had banded together to promote their unique museums situated along a hundred-mile stretch of state Highway 14. The variety represented was surprising. I'd expected traditional small-town historical museums that would be pretty similar to each other, but as I looked at the brochure, I found myself looking forward to visiting all of them. From the Campbell Straw Bale Built Museum in Carthage to the Loriks-Peterson Heritage House Museum in Oldham and the South Dakota Amateur Baseball Hall of Fame in Lake Norden, each promised an enlightening experience.

Fortunately, nearly every town across America has its own historical landmarks and special features. You just need to find them. Start your research by visiting your town's website. Many have links to local points of interest, upcoming events, and your local tourism council. Your Chamber of Commerce or Visitors and Convention Bureau are both excellent sources of information and are often linked to the town's website. Most towns have an organization focused on tourism, and they'll be happy to recommend activities. You can also visit your local library to find books about the town's history or check tourist guidebooks for mentions of nearby destinations. And AAA Travel has information on many areas, including small-town points of interest.

Once you start researching, you may be surprised by what you find. One discovery may lead to another, and the next thing you know, you have a deeper appreciation for the town's origins and why the first residents settled there. Or you may discover a significant contribution to art or a noteworthy invention tied to your town's history or even a connection that goes much further back.

Historical Locations and Monuments

North American history goes back thousands of years, to a time long before immigrants had settled the United States. Every region has an interesting history and a story to tell, and this history is preserved through monuments, historic sites, and national landmarks that are as fascinating to visit for residents as they are for tourists. Being a hometown tourist is fun whether you've lived somewhere your whole life or you recently relocated. Either way, the adventure of discovery is most rewarding when you take your time to enjoy and learn about everything that makes your town special.

When I moved to Baltimore, one of the first landmarks I visited was Fort McHenry. It's the site of the famous battle in 1814 that inspired Francis Scott Key to write *The Star-Spangled Banner*. Like most Americans, I'd memorized that song in elementary school and had been singing it my entire life, but the sobering impact of the words didn't hit me until I stood at the fort, looking out at the harbor where Key would have been as he watched the battle.

An attorney who boarded a British ship to negotiate the release of American prisoners, Key was not permitted to leave, because the British believed that he'd disclose critical details of the British force to the Americans. He was forced to watch the subsequent battle from the deck, fearful of what was happening to his country. All night, he strained to see details each time the sky was briefly lit up during the bombings. Once the sun finally rose and he saw the American flag flying over the fort, he was overcome with pride and relief.

As I stood on the spot that Key had strained to see as he waited to learn the outcome of this pivotal battle, the anthem took on a deeper meaning for me. It's been more than ten years since I visited Fort McHenry, but to this day every time I hear *The Star Spangled Banner*, I relive that moment and feel the same level of reverence and patriotism in the song's words.

When you start learning the history of a location, you find that there are lots of stories behind the events that occurred there. Being a local tourist allows you to learn and appreciate more of the history because you can visit a point of interest again and again. There are many spots I've visited while traveling that I wished I'd had more time to explore: The Alamo in San Antonio, the Buffalo Bill Center of the West museum complex in Cody, Wyoming, the James River Plantations, and Williamsburg, Virginia, to name a few. When we set out to learn about an area, we not only find nearby gems but we also get to experience the thrill of exploration.

Parks & Nature Preserves

One of the best things about being a local tourist is becoming a member of parks, nature preserves, and botanical gardens. You can visit all the natural attractions your area has to offer and join the ones you want to visit again. In warm weather, pack a picnic basket and head to one of your favorite parks or preserves. Whether you go by yourself to enjoy the serenity of nature or you invite a friend for a leisurely lunch, it's a mini-vacation.

Many towns have nature centers that are on a tourist's must-see list. Dallas has the six thousand-acre Trinity River Audubon Center, Seattle boasts the Seward Park Audubon Center, and right outside Santa Barbara you can spend the day walking around more than nine acres at the Coronado Butterfly Preserve. What spot close to you is a popular tourist destination?

Tourist Attractions

Be sure to take advantage of activities geared toward tourists, such as guided ghost-town tours. Many businesses rely on the tourist trade, so they work hard to make the activities fun. Take a tour of a local winery or indulge in a hot air balloon ride and see your town from a whole new perspective. And check for discounts from an online coupon site such as Groupon or Living Social. Both are excellent resources for finding the fun spots, and you can snag discount passes for sports events, miniatures golf, water parks, and even bed-and-breakfast packages.

Did you know that many businesses offer tours even if they don't promote them? Some car manufacturing plants, dairies, sawmills, and even candy-making companies offer visitors an inside look at their operations. A website called Factory Tours USA (www.factorytoursusa.com) provides information on more than five hundred tours available, but it's not a complete list. Don't be afraid to call and see if an interesting business in your area offers tours.

Art, Theater & Museums

Vacations are a time to have new experiences and step out of your comfort zone. Take a vacation day from your normal routine and be a hometown tourist at a local play, a high school band concert, or an art gallery. It may be something you never want to repeat, but at least do it once for the experience.

Make a point to visit local museums. Most major cities have large art museums, but smaller towns have impressive collections as well, like the Redlin Art Center in Watertown, South Dakota, which houses more than 150 original paintings by artist Terry Redlin. The Ohr-O'Keefe Museum in Biloxi, Mississippi, showcases the ceramic pottery of George E. Ohr and several other artists.

There are unusual collections in specialty museums all around the country that should be on any hometown tourist list. Phoenix has the Musical Instrument Museum, with more than fifteen hundred items from two hundred countries, and the Huntington in San Marino, California, offers lush botanical gardens and a library of rare books and manuscripts, including a Gutenberg Bible from the 1450s. From the Farragut Folklife Museum in Tennessee to the Mystic Seaport Museum in Connecticut, which features a re-creation of an entire nineteenth-century seaport village, to the Wallace Mining Museum in Idaho, museums in every part of the country have stories to tell.

Have you ever wanted to do something you thought would be fun but didn't do it because you couldn't find someone to join you? Let's agree to not let that happen again. There's no reason that the lack of a companion should stop us from visiting someplace new. In most cases, if we're enjoying a park, a museum, or a gallery alone, no one will take a second look. Likely, no one will care or find it odd if we're alone. The same can apply to plays, concerts, or an evening meal at a restaurant you've been wanting to try. It's okay to go somewhere alone. Let's not worry about what other people think. Exploring and enjoying new places by ourselves is fun and empowering. It's our hometown—let's go out and experience everything it has to offer!

THE CHALLENGE
TAKE A FRESH LOOK
AT YOUR HOMETOWN

"One's destination is never a place,
but rather a new way of looking at things."
—Henry Miller, American author

How long have you lived in your hometown? Have you been to all the tourist stops and interesting locations? Stop by the local tourism office and pick up a brochure to read. Challenge yourself to find new activities to take part in and places to visit in your hometown or county. Other people travel to see what you have access to every day. Take advantage of the treasures nearby.

CHALLENGE CHECKLIST

☐ Visit a local art museum.

☐ Attend a play or a production by a local dance group.

☐ Visit a cultural museum or historic center.

☐ Have a picnic at a local park.

☐ Attend a game of your local sports team.

☐ Try a local independent restaurant.

☐ Find the number one tourist spot in your area and spend a day there.

☐ Visit a specialty store or souvenir shop.

☐ Spend the afternoon at a local zoo or animal preserve.

☐ Take a hike on a popular trail.

☐ Book an overnight stay at a local B&B.

☐ Go to the symphony or ballet.

10

Enjoy the Simple Things

they're not only fun—

they're often free!

"The best things in life aren't things."
—Art Buchwald, American humorist

Who doesn't enjoy a morning cup of coffee in the garden, a comfortable pair of shoes, or settling down with a good book? The simple things in life can often bring us the most enjoyment.

We've all heard the adage "Stop and smell the roses." It's a mantra that reminds us to slow down and enjoy life's simple pleasures. That reminder might be needed more in our younger years, when we're sometimes overwhelmed by the challenges of balancing career and family. But as we age, the thought of enjoying simple things doesn't always sound appealing. It might even sound downright boring. While we look forward to slowing down and relaxing when we're working full time, after we retire it often represents the onset of a sedentary life without challenges or new experiences. That's the opposite of what we need to stay young.

I've always loved to hike trails through wooded areas. Before I retired, I often retreated to the serenity of nature —the hushed sounds under the canopy of trees, echoing bird songs, the crackling underbrush as unseen critters scurried by. In the forest, I felt far away from my human concerns and to-do lists. Being surrounded by nature was a simple pleasure that helped me relax and clear my mind. But once I retired from my high-stress career, the way I experienced nature changed. Wanting my time outside to be invigorating, I often kept up a brisk pace while still appreciating the peace and serenity of the natural environment. Since I had more time for hiking, I frequently chose a park that has seven miles of hiking trails with varying degrees of difficulty, from easy to strenuous.

At Forest Park Nature Center in Peoria, Illinois, I encountered a welcome challenge when I learned about its hundred-mile hikers club. It takes a simple pleasure and turns it into a challenge: hike just one mile a day for four months to reach the goal. Once you reach the milestone, you receive a reward to commemorate the accomplishment. At Forest Park, you earn a T-shirt for reaching 100 miles, a patch for 250 miles, and a lapel pin at 500 miles. As for me, I'm still working towards my T-shirt. Many parks throughout the United States offer similar programs, like Yellowstone National Park, which offers a T-shirt, a key chain, and a certificate at different levels of achievement.

In retirement, we have more time to enjoy the simple things in life, but we also have more time to take hobbies and interests to a new level. If baking is your passion, instead of making a dozen cookies for your countertop cookie jar, bake five dozen and share them with your neighbors. The next time you have a morning doctor's appointment or meeting with your accountant, take along a dozen homemade muffins. That's just one way the little things we enjoy can be expanded into more significant activities.

There are countless ways to embrace and fully appreciate the extra time we have to indulge in the activities we enjoy most. What activities bring you the most contentment or pleasure? Whatever they are, there are ways to enhance them to make them even more engaging:

- If you enjoy playing card games with friends, organize an activity for a larger group: bring together a dozen people for a bunco night or set up a contract bridge tournament or poker game.

- Offer to plan all the details of a birthday party or a family dinner party, from theme research to entertainment, decorations, music, and food. Use online sites for checklists and ideas.

- If you like to bake or cook, enter baking contests or sign up to cook at your local church or nonprofit events.

- If you enjoy reading, read for story time at the library.

- If you like walking, join a walking or hiking club at the local park.

- If you're a fan of sunrises and sunsets, take photographs of them and share on social media or in contests.

Our five senses are designed to help us appreciate everything in our environment. Sight, hearing, smell, taste, and touch are readily available to savor any moment, and these sensations are often the things we associate with the simple pleasures of life. Everyone has small things that bring them a sense of contentment and peace—enjoying a glass of wine in the evening, watching squirrels playing in the trees, the smell of the grass after a summer rain. It's different for everyone, but the simple things are often free and may not even require special equipment to enjoy.

Labor of Love
simple pleasures can turn into passions

"Passion is energy. Feel the power that comes from focusing on what excites you."
—Oprah Winfrey, American actress and talk show host

For thirty years I worked as a consultant in telecommunications, where high-stress is part of every day. Like many people, I liked to manage my stress by visualizing a retirement without pressure, a simple life that would make all the years of long hours worthwhile. When I transitioned from consultant to writer, I was able to start building that lifestyle while working from home, continuing to earn a living while enjoying more simple pleasures.

Without having any idea how much work would be involved, I decided to plant my first garden. Tilling and preparing the ground was the first step, followed by deciding what to plant. I knew I wanted to raise vegetables, not flowers, but I needed quite a bit of education before I was ready to plant anything. I settled on tomatoes, green peppers, jalapeños, zucchini, corn, carrots, and okra. Each one had different requirements for distance between plants, depth of seed planting, and even how long they would take to grow.

Unfortunately, I forgot to keep a record, and after a month I was forced to post a photo of a plant to an online group for identification because I had no idea what it was. But I kept at it. I weeded and watered and watched everything grow, loving the daily exercise and fresh air. Near the end of the summer, I felt a sense of satisfaction and accomplishment every day when I was able to harvest my crops.

When autumn came, my vegetable harvest was dwindling, but my apple tree was heavy with big, ripe fruit. I never realized how many apples one tree could produce and was quickly overwhelmed by the sheer quantity. After discarding the ones with bruises or worms, I still had more than four hundred apples. A typical apple pie uses about six large apples, so I was obviously going to have to find other uses for them.

I was unprepared for the amount of work that goes into canning apple pie filling, but I learned fast and made more than forty quarts. I made muffins, breads, and cakes, and I chopped and froze thirty pounds of blanched apples and made three dozen jars of apple butter. As good as the pie filling was, the apple butter was my crowning achievement. My grandmother made the best apple butter, another simple pleasure and one of the best memories from my childhood. Unfortunately, she passed away when I was a teenager, and I never found her recipe. But I found one that almost makes itself, right in a Crock-Pot, with about thirty minutes' work. I use a stainless steel Johnny Apple Slicer, which is a nifty gadget that peels, cores, and slices the apples all at the same time, making the apple preparation a breeze. I bought mine at a local kitchen store, but they're readily available at online retailers, usually for under twenty dollars.

There are many varieties of apples available, each with different textures, flavors, and levels of juiciness. To learn which apples are best for each purpose, I went to one of my favorite sources: *The Farmers' Almanac*. Its online articles and guides cover many topics, and gardening is one of the big ones. While there's room for personal preference and certainly mixing different varieties in a recipe, there are some general considerations to keep in mind. The best apples for snacking are usually those that are crisp and juicy and have a mild flavor, such as Cortland, Golden Delicious, and Honeycrisp. Baking apples should be firm, so that they won't get overly soft when cooked, and somewhat sweet. Fuji and Granny

Smith are good choices for baking. For apple butter, applesauce, or cooking, you'll want an apple that's softer and will cook down to a smoother consistency. Softer varieties include McIntosh, Red Delicious, and Jonathan. I'm not sure what variety our tree is, but I found that our apples are well-suited for baking and apple butter, and they work best for pie and cobblers when I mix them with crisp varieties.

On the following page is my apple butter recipe, using my home-grown apples from a hybrid tree.

Crock-Pot Apple Butter

About 3 pounds of apples
(about 12-15 medium-size)
3 cups sugar
2 tsp. cinnamon
1 tsp. nutmeg
¼ tsp. allspice
¼ tsp. cloves
⅛ tsp. salt
¾ cup apple cider
(may substitute water)

1. Wash and peel the apples, removing the core and slice thin, into one-inch chunks

2. In a small bowl, mix the sugar and spices.

3. Put half the apples in the crockpot and sprinkle with half the sugar and spice mix.

4. Add the remaining apples and cover with the remaining sugar and spice mix.

5. Pour apple juice over the entire thing. Use a large spoon to mix a bit.

6. Set the crockpot to low and cook about nine hours (you can set it to cook overnight).

7. It's ready when it has a thick spreadable consistency. You can use a wire whisk to break up larger pieces, but gently because it will be very hot.

Makes about 48 ounces. Store in the refrigerator for several weeks or preserve with water-bath canning. To can, pack into six eight-ounce jars using ¼-inch headspace. Can in hot water bath for 10 minutes.

THE CHALLENGE
CREATE ACTIVITY
AROUND A SIMPLE PLEASURE

"That man is rich whose pleasures are the cheapest."
—Henry David Thoreau, American author

Think about the simple things that you enjoy or that you enjoyed before you retired. How can you turn those free, simple indulgences into engaging activities? Challenge yourself to find more simple pleasures and enjoy them with a little more gusto.

CHALLENGE CHECKLIST

☐ Go apple-picking and make your favorite recipes to enjoy and share.

☐ Read a new book recommended by a local book club and share your impressions.

☐ Share a laugh with a friend by having a monthly night out at a comedy club.

☐ Watch the sunset or sunrise and share photos or use the photos to inspire a painting.

☐ Invite children over for a cookie-baking class.

☐ Participate in a hundred-mile club challenge.

☐ Organize recipes and make an online scrapbook to share.

☐ Set up and maintain a free library box (https:// littlefreelibrary.org).

☐ Pick fresh flowers for your home and make extra arrangements to give to a neighbor or a nursing home resident.

☐ Organize a knitting or quilting circle and donate the creations to a community project.

☐ Use your hobbies to make gifts, like ceramics or woodworking projects.

☐ Attend a dance once a month.

11

Explore Nature
it's right outside your door

> "In all things of nature
> there is something of the marvelous."
> —Aristotle

Remember when you were stuck inside as a kid? Rainy days, lightning, and snowstorms forced us inside, and even if it was only for a day, it could feel like the walls were closing in around us. It turns out that that claustrophobic feeling can be as strong when we're adults as it was when we were kids. No matter our age, being housebound can make us a little stir crazy.

Science explains why we crave being outside. Studies have shown that a surprising range of medical benefits are gained from the simple act of taking a walk or just sitting on the porch. Being outside, especially around greenery, can help improve our mood, attention span, and even memory. A Harvard University study showed that people who lived near trees and plants lived an average of twelve years longer. The research didn't find a single location in America where that wasn't true. The idea that spending time in nature improves health isn't new, but recent studies have shown that the benefits are broader than we once thought.

It's Good for Our Mind

The University of Pittsburgh studied the benefit of sunlight and found that it can reduce both stress and physical pain. Sunlight is good for our memory, too. A study at the University of Michigan found that as little as one hour spent in a natural setting helped people improve their memory and attention span by 20 percent, and it significantly lowered depression.

It's Good for Our Body

Did you know that 80 to 90 percent of our body's vitamin D intake comes from the sun? Vitamin D helps reduce our risk of rheumatoid arthritis, osteoporosis, and even a heart attack. Fresh air also helps produce white blood cells to battle viruses and inflammation, and it improves overall cardiovascular and metabolic health. Many people are deficient in vitamin D because they don't get enough sunshine, and while sunscreen protects us from UV rays it also blocks much-needed vitamin D, so your doctor may recommend you add foods rich in vitamin D to your diet or even take vitamin D supplements.

It's Good for Our Spirit

Spending just twenty minutes a day outside has been shown to significantly boost vitality levels, energy, and a sense of well-being. A University of Rochester study found that nature, more than any other stimulus, increased energy and vitality within the research group. Another study, published in the *Journal of Health and Aging*, found that seventy-year-olds who spent time outdoors reported less pain and had less trouble sleeping.

Fresh Air and Sunshine
mom was right—it's good for you

"There is new life in the soil for every man.
There is healing in the trees for tired minds
and for our overburdened spirits,
there is strength in the hills,
if only we will lift up our eyes.
Remember that nature is your great restorer."
—Calvin Coolidge, thirtieth president of the United States

Nearly three-quarters of Americans over sixty-five live in metropolitan areas, making access to green spaces challenging. In rural areas, simply spending time in the backyard provides the health and wellness benefits of nature. But if you live in an urban setting or a senior community, you may have to get creative to incorporate nature into your daily activity. Either way, it often makes sense to start adding more outdoor time to your schedule while staying close to home.

If you have a yard, start a vegetable or flower garden. You can make it as large or small as you like, and you'll have the added benefit of fresh flowers or vegetables after a few months. If you don't have a yard or it isn't big enough, check to see if there's a community garden in your area. Local senior centers and beautification groups may be able to help you find one.

A popular option for people who live in cities is the strip of grass or dirt between the road and the sidewalk, sometimes called a "hellstrip." This strip is often a legal no-man's-land, owned by the local municipality but not maintained by it, leaving the care and maintenance to the closest property owner. Many cities allow residents to turn these neglected swaths into planting areas. Check your local city government ordinances to see if hellstrip planting is allowed and what criteria you need to follow.

If gardening isn't a possibility or doesn't sound appealing, think about other activities you can enjoy outside. If you have artistic leanings, set up a space outdoors and paint or sketch the landscape for an hour a day. If you'd rather not spend time alone, many outdoor activities can be done with a friend or a group. Activities like fishing and bird-watching can be fun ways for people to enjoy nature together. The Audubon Society has more than 450 local chapters where you can attend events, learn about birds, and get involved in conservation efforts while you enjoy the outdoors.

Sports are another fun way to combine socializing and outdoor activity. While golf takes time and practice to master, it's easy to learn the basics, and the same is true for many other sports, from softball to pickleball to cycling. Check with your local parks and recreation department or community center to find organized activities that combine physical activity with sunshine and fresh air. If you can't find a group that matches your interests, consider starting one.

If you have grandchildren living nearby, take them along for some playground time. The fresh air benefits everyone, and you have the added bonus of making memories. Or simply take a walk in a nearby park to appreciate nature in many forms. To savor a beautiful day, take a book along, find a bench, and read for a while. Taking a dog on a walk, whether it's your own pup or a friend's, can make the walk more entertaining and amusing. I found that out firsthand after an energetic schnoodle joined my household.

While I've always enjoyed walks through wooded areas and nature preserves simply to appreciate nature, as I reached my late forties and early fifties I looked forward to the physical activity as much as the relaxation time. Once my dog, Dusty, and later her puppy, Thor, joined me, I gained a new level of awareness. They investigate every scent and explore every little spot as if it's the first time they've ever been there, even on the hundredth trip, because every time is just a little bit different. They've taught me to appreciate every experience and notice the little things.

When I lived in Illinois, my favorite spot was a square of green that boasted a small lake with a fishing dock, located right outside the town of Tremont. I visited that park nearly every day, taking my two dogs on the mile-long circle around the water. The water's edge was thick with tall grass and trees, and the dogs would rush toward the water, sniffing and snuffling, often disturbing birds, squirrels, and rabbits with their noisy excitement. Rarely were there any other people at the park, save the occasional fisherman.

After a few hundred feet, the shoreline cut in, and the trees opened up for access to a fishing spot where a bench and a fire pit with a grill sat close to the water. It was a comfortable spot to enjoy the sunlight sparkling on the water or, if it was late in the evening, the reds, oranges, and purples of the sunset that reflected off the surface. The park is situated lower than the surrounding area, so the air was often still, and the ripples in the water were signs of fish, insects, birds, or other wildlife. I have at least twenty photos of sunsets at that lake. Once we passed the fishing bench, we would walk into a little-used area of the park and I'd let out the full twenty feet of the retractable leashes, allowing the dogs more freedom to explore. They knew the routine as we circled the lake, staying a few feet away from the shoreline as we walked.

Every day something was different. After a rain shower, the air was crisp and clean, with an underlying earthy scent from the ground. Other days, the scent of freshly cut grass filled the air. There were no flowers there, only thick grass that grew up to the water's edge, where it blended with taller reeds at the bank. I was fascinated by how different the park could look, depending on whether it was sunny or cloudy, and how the sunlight streamed through the tree leaves at midday and gave everything a golden glow at dusk and dawn. But the highlight was the wildlife—catching a glimpse of a muskrat or a mink, hearing a great horned owl hoot, watching a mama duck with a line of little ducklings trailing after her in a way that always made me laugh. Occasionally we'd see geese, and once we even saw a beaver. On humid summer evenings, as the sun started setting, I could hear fish splashing and plopping at the surface of the lake as they were drawn up by the buzzing insects. On those nights, the whine of the mosquitoes kept me moving at a brisk pace to stave off their attacks. And then there were the windy and chilly days, when the park seemed almost desolate, as if no animals lived there at all.

Whether I felt like walking or not, I always left the park in a better mood than when I arrived. I used to think of this spot as magical, but in my travels throughout the United States, I've learned that the magic isn't in the location— it's in nature itself.

THE CHALLENGE

EXPLORE THE
LOCAL LANDSCAPE

"Nature is better than a middling doctor."
—Chinese proverb

When we think about nature, we might tend to imagine a national park with miles of forests. But nature is in the local park, too, and even in your backyard. Surrounding yourself with nature is as easy as surrounding yourself with living green plants. What can you challenge yourself with to add more time with nature to your life?

CHALLENGE CHECKLIST

- ☐ Go for a walk every day.

- ☐ Plant a garden or a few flowers outside.

- ☐ Choose outdoor or patio seating at a restaurant.

- ☐ Try an outdoor hobby like bird-watching or fishing.

- ☐ Go camping for the weekend.

☐ Have a picnic at a local park.

☐ Go canoeing or kayaking.

☐ Visit an arboretum or botanical garden.

☐ Go for a hike at a local state or national park.

☐ Go for a bicycle ride.

☐ Enjoy the sunset from the deck or the front porch.

☐ Bring nature inside in the form of plants or an herb garden.

12

Be Bold

be willing to take a chance

"The bold and the generous have the best lives."
—Icelandic proverb

Why is riding on a roller coaster fun? Why do some people seek the adrenaline rush of paragliding or zip-lining? The heights, the speed, even feeling out of control can be scary in a good way.

As we get older, activities we've always enjoyed can seem mundane or even boring. When that happens, it might be time to take a chance and try something new, even if that something is a little scary. Science tells us that adrenaline is the body's natural response to fear, but the chemicals released along with the adrenaline can give us a feeling of euphoria. Some people are quick to embrace this excitement, while others are more likely to hesitate.

My mother was always one to embrace it. Maybe it was her Scandinavian heritage and innate Viking spirit that made her so adventurous, but whatever the reason, she welcomed every opportunity and raised all ten of us to welcome it, too. Once during a family reunion in Colorado, we eagerly rafted the white water of the Upper Animas River. Mom was seventy, but she pulled her weight with the paddle, helping to ensure that her boat didn't capsize in the strong rapids. She thrived on thrills, so none of us raised an eyebrow when, eighteen years later, one of my sisters bought her a tandem paragliding experience for her eighty-eighth birthday. I have to admit I did raise an eyebrow when I watched her and her instructor performing flips in midair, but she loved every minute of it. So it was no surprise when Mom made arrangements to paraglide again two years later, this time in Iceland. She was giddy with excitement, and the excitement was infectious, so I agreed to go with her and try paragliding myself.

It's an interesting thing sometimes, to think about what we're afraid of or intimidated by. I'm comfortable speaking to audiences of several hundred people and even relish the excitement of white-water rafting, but paragliding was an entirely different experience. My discomfort with heights and the sensation of unfettered midair flight combined to make the experience one that I'd hesitate to repeat.

For some people, being bold means facing a physical challenge or fear. Others are more apprehensive about speaking in public or performing in front of a group. Regardless of the source of fears, there are benefits to facing and overcoming them. I may never go paragliding again, but I'm glad I did it at least once and cherish the experience. The memory of the flight, the amazing views from that height, and the camaraderie of having the shared adventure with my mom are all part of why I don't regret doing it.

In addition to helping us become more self-confident, overcoming fears can help us to be more empathetic to others with similar apprehensions and open a whole new world of events and activities. If you're uncomfortable with public speaking, volunteer to read for children's story hour—as an audience, they're a lot more forgiving of nervousness and can help build your confidence about taking on even bigger challenges later. If the idea of performing feels intimidating, consider auditioning for a small role at your local theater or take on a support role like serving as an usher or working on set design. Community theater groups open new doors for socializing and growing your circle of friends.

No matter what fears or uncertainties are limiting our activities, we can confront them and often surmount them by starting small. If you've always wanted to take a cruise but are afraid of water, take the first step by signing up for swimming lessons or water safety. If you're not comfortable asking that special someone out on a first date, invite them to join you for a walk or a cup of coffee. There's an abundance of benefits when we resolve to be bold and take the first step.

Remember, the mind is as resilient as the body. To become stronger physically, we follow a workout and gradually increase the difficulty. Our minds can work the same way. Start small and build the challenge gradually. You might find yourself enjoying many activities you never thought you'd try. And even if your greatest public speaking engagement is reading for story time or you decide to stay off the main stage, being bold will expand your world in delightfully unexpected ways.

Test Your Limits
you'll never know until you try

"Action may not always bring happiness,
but there is no happiness without action."
—William James, American philosopher and psychologist

The concept of boldness and the idea of testing our limits are topics usually reserved for motivation in physical fitness and business. In both areas, we learn how to assess risk, establish priorities, and measure success. We work toward achieving a goal—biking ten miles, finishing a marathon, closing the sale, getting the promotion. At the gym, we grit our teeth and push for one more rep. At the office, we take on a challenging project to prove to the boss we're up to the task.

In retirement, instead of giving up that way of thinking, we can apply it to other endeavors. There is no maximum age for new experiences and no expiration date for a challenge. To truly reach life's full potential, we should never stop pushing ourselves toward something new. Testing our limits helps us determine what we're fully capable of, whether that's a physical accomplishment, a mental challenge, or a leadership achievement in a group.

When I was forty-six, I had the opportunity to do just that. Back in elementary school, I'd harbored a secret dream of joining the Air Force to fly planes, maybe even pilot the space shuttle one day, but I told myself that since my eyesight was poor, it was something I could never do, so I never pursued it. Honestly, it probably had more to do with my nervousness about heights than anything else. Not a fear exactly but strong discomfort. Then one day about thirty-five years later, I was visiting my mom at her home when her friend Marvin, who was a private pilot, called. Marvin often called on friends to sit in the co-pilot's seat and keep him company when he needed to fly somewhere, but Mom had plans that day and couldn't go, so she suggested I might like to. I was a little scared but also excited, so I thought, *Why not?*

I met Marvin at a small private airport and we flew to a town about forty miles away. He kept up a constant stream of chatter, explaining each task as he performed it—a natural teacher who clearly enjoyed having an interested student. He explained the operation of the plane and pointed out the instruments and controls, telling me about how they worked and the functions they performed. He taught me about the dials and the gauges and used unfamiliar words like *altimeter* and *gyroscope.*

Marvin's passion for flying was so infectious that when he offered me the controls, I boldly accepted. And after just one minute behind the stick, I was hooked. It was even more exciting than my first time behind the wheel of a car. I'm not sure why I loved piloting a small craft but didn't enjoy paragliding, but I did. Maybe it was because the twin-engine Cessna 414A was big enough to feel stable and small enough to feel free.

Today, years later, I can close my eyes and I'm back in the co-pilot's seat, looking out at the expanse of sky and the green fields below, bisected with gray strips of paved road and brown lines of dirt road. We were the only witnesses to the scene around us, and I remember feeling blessed to be privy to such a beautiful sight. I remember feeling the sun on my face and seeing a few puffy clouds high in the sky above us, providing a stark white contrast to the vivid blue sky. The memory feels almost as surreal and peaceful as being in the plane felt.

Boldness isn't necessarily courageous or heroic. It's a *willingness* to act with confidence or to take a risk. It's confronting fear or insecurity and not allowing it to limit our life experiences.

THE CHALLENGE
FACE FEAR AND INSECURITY

"Freedom lies in being bold."
—Robert Frost, American poet

Think about what fears or uncertainties may be holding you back from something you've always wanted to do. Is there a first step you can take? Adding a little boldness to life can lead to lots of adventures.

CHALLENGE CHECKLIST

☐ Ride on a roller coaster or a zip line.

☐ Take a tandem paragliding or parasailing ride.

☐ Join a theater group.

☐ Visit a water park or a beach.

☐ Learn to swim.

☐ Volunteer to organize or emcee an event.

☐ Spearhead a charitable or nonprofit event.

☐ Join a singles group or go on a first date.

☐ Share poetry or personal writing with a group.

☐ Take a ride in a hot air balloon.

☐ Visit an animal sanctuary.

☐ Sing a song at karaoke.

13

Be Playful

stay young at heart

"Age is an issue of mind over matter.
If you don't mind, it doesn't matter."
—Mark Twain, American author

What does the phrase *young at heart* mean to you? For some people it means staying current with fashion trends, for others it's about focusing on physical fitness, and for some it's a mind-set of happiness and joy. When the *Chicago Tribune* asked a dozen people older than sixty-three what being young at heart meant to them, their responses ranged from "a way of life that is active, hope-filled, giving and unburdened by regrets" to "living on your own terms and trying new things." There isn't a universal answer to the question.

For me, being young at heart means embracing life with exuberance, being optimistic, and never being afraid to play. For children, playing is the most natural thing in the world. It's what we did, almost unconsciously. As adults, after years of work, routine, and responsibility, we sometimes forget how to play. But even if the pure joy of having fun is a distant memory, you can choose to start playing again, right here and now. Getting older doesn't mean we should stop having fun. We can decide to cut loose, be silly, and just live in the moment again, like we did when we were kids.

We all have our own idea of fun, so there's no right or wrong activity. The important thing to remember is that true play can be anything we do for the sole purpose of relaxing or having fun. Do you remember playing hand-clapping games like Miss Mary Mack? Did you ever walk to the water's edge to skip stones? Or spend hours doing tricks with a hula hoop or jumping on a pogo stick? When we were children, these activities were part of everyday life. As adults, we often have to remind ourselves that it's okay to play, laugh, and joke around and that, in fact, it's healthy.

Too often we avoid play because we're self-conscious about looking silly, especially as we get older. But rarely if ever do we look at, say, an older couple on the dance floor and think they look silly. We're more likely to smile and nod, thinking *I want to be just like that.* I'm often a vendor at Scandinavian festivals, where I have a booth with a backdrop featuring a Viking ship and a head-in-the-hole photo stand. Festival participants have photos taken with their heads on a Viking's body, standing in front of a classic longboat. I designed it with children in mind, making sure the hole for the head was about four feet off the ground. I never imagined how many adults would jump behind the board to have a photo taken. Even though they have to squat to peer through the hole, they don't hesitate. They're often laughing as they finagle the awkward pose, and the pure childlike joy on the faces of people playing make-believe brings a smile to my own face every time. I'll never forget the time an elderly woman insisted on a photo and her family members helped her from a wheelchair and supported her as I took a photo for them.

I love knowing that playing doesn't have an age limit. Even into her nineties, my mom followed her impulses to engage in silliness and playtime. She used to say she couldn't be expected to act her age because she'd never been that age before and she might as well just have fun. Most people were surprised to learn her age, which could have been because of her agility and how physically active she was, but I think her constant playfulness deserved a lot of the credit.

When she was eighty-nine, we visited an open-air museum, the Árbær, in Reykjavik, and Mom remembered many of the pieces in its toy collection from her childhood. As we left the museum, she gasped and pointed to several pairs of stilts leaning against the outside wall of the building. Before I could even guess what might happen next, she rushed over, pulled a couple of them upright, and hopped up to get her right foot on the peg. Within seconds, two museum employees appeared out of thin air and supported her on both sides. They looked nervous, but she had a huge grin on her face as she took a couple of wobbly steps. The surrounding crowd didn't concern her, and neither did the fact that she was wearing her "church clothes" and two-inch heels. Of course, people stopped to watch, but based on the big smiles on their faces, I don't think anyone thought she was silly. I think her playfulness was heartwarming.

We can all make time for play, with the only goal being to laugh and have fun. Don't be afraid of letting that inner child out. If you're out of practice, don't worry about it—the more you play, the easier it becomes. Before long, playing will be as spontaneous as it was when you were young. Opportunities to have fun are all around us. Practice spotting the stilts in life and you'll never be bored.

It doesn't matter whether they're indoor or outdoor activities—discover things that are fun for you and do them as often as you can. Here are some ideas to get your wheels turning:

- Paddleboating on a lake
- Board games
- Cards and dice games
- Coloring books

- Building models

- Miniature golf

- Go-carts

- Kite-flying

While there are plenty of enjoyable activities we can do alone, the idea of playfulness usually makes people think of time with friends and family, so it's not surprising that many adults seek out play as a way to enhance social connection. Sometimes it's easier to be spontaneous when we're with other people. When we're all being silly, we don't feel self-conscious.

Playing Games for Fun
it's not about winning

"We don't stop playing because we grow old;
we grow old because we stop playing."
—George Bernard Shaw, Irish playwright

Playtime is good for us because it adds joy to life. The expression "Laughter is the best medicine" has a lot of truth to it. Research dating back centuries shows that laughter helps to relieve stress, reduce pain, and lower blood pressure. Plus, it produces those euphoric endor-phins that are natural mood enhancers. The mental stimulation of playing games also supports healthy brain function. Studies show that spending as little as five or ten minutes a day on games or puzzles helps us to stay mentally sharp.

If you're out of practice and need some help, spend time with playful people. Children are especially good at playing. If you can, set aside time to play with children, and don't be afraid to follow their lead—dance through the sprinklers, join in a game of Simon Says, play hide-and-go-seek. Ask them to teach you their favorite game and give it your full attention. You'll never know how much fun Hungry Hungry Hippos is until you really work to win.

Instead of relying only on spontaneous opportunities for playing, why not make it a priority and plan time for it? Invite a friend to join you at bingo, or find a local spot that has trivia night or even karaoke. You can find these events by checking out community bulletin boards, local event calendars, and websites for senior centers. In the autumn and winter, outdoor activities are more limited but social leagues for indoor sports and games like bowling and darts are just getting started. A typical season for a weekly bowling league is about eight months. Dart league season usually runs three to four months.

If you'd rather stay closer to home, organize a card game with friends and neighbors. Pinochle, bridge, canasta, rummy, and cribbage are all popular card games that provide fun challenges, and you can play them with four or more players. If you're more in the mood for socializing than concentrating, set up a game night with dice games like LRC (Left, Right, Center) or Yahtzee. What or how you choose to play is far less important than making playfulness part of every day.

If you're still thinking you're too old to play, think about this: how old would you be if you didn't know how old you were? No matter how many birthdays you've celebrated or how long it's been since you've allowed yourself to be childlike, you can always revive your playful spirit. Reconnect with your inner child, who isn't at all afraid to be silly and have fun. Tell an unexpected joke or make a funny face the next time someone snaps a photo. When we approach life with a smile and keep playing, we'll always be young at heart.

THE CHALLENGE
BE PLAYFUL JUST FOR FUN

"Just play. Have fun. Enjoy the game."
—Michael Jordan, American basketball star

We think of playtime as something for children. You might even think it's a frivolous waste of time. It's not. Making time for fun and allowing yourself time to play brings joy into your life. Challenge yourself to find an activity that can make you smile, even laugh, every day.

CHALLENGE CHECKLIST

☐ Have your face painted at a carnival.

☐ Fly a kite.

☐ Go to an amusement park.

☐ Swing on the swings at a park.

☐ Take a spin on a go-cart.

☐ Finger-paint.

☐ Go to a ball pit playroom (they have adult ones!).

☐ Join a league for bowling, darts, or any other sport.

☐ Go for a ride in a four-wheeler.

☐ Play a children's game.

☐ Include a piñata at your next party.

☐ Have a pillow fight or a water gun battle.

14

Just Keep Moving
bodies in motion stay in motion

"Age is no barrier.
It's a limitation you put on your mind."
—Jackie Joyner-Kersee, American Olympic medalist

Movement isn't just about getting exercise. The human body needs basic activity and movement to function correctly. Movement supports blood circulation, digestion, and metabolism. We've all felt the tense muscles and lethargy that set in after we've been sitting too long—my mom used to call it "sit-itis." A sedentary lifestyle leads to joint stiffness, loss of bone density, and the weakening of muscles, including those that support heart and lung function.

What's most important for us to remember is that no matter our age, if we take good care of ourselves, we can be active and enjoy life. My mom once told me a story that drove this point home. She was driving on a country road in Minnesota when she saw an old Ford Model T rusting in a field. Judging by the abundance of weeds growing around the metal skeleton, she figured it had been there a long time. As luck would have it, a few miles later, when she stopped at a traffic light, another Model T pulled up in the lane next to her. This one was impeccable —sea-green paint smoothly covered the exterior, the white-wall tires were spotless, and the chrome gleamed. She said she couldn't help but compare the car she'd seen rusting quietly in the field with the one next to her, all shiny, oiled up, and roaring with life.

The story is an accurate analogy for life. Sometimes, especially in retirement, it's easy to slide into a sedentary lifestyle and, quite frankly, get rusty. As Mom would say, don't let your body "rust up"—it's the only one you have. If you want it to keep going, you'd better keep it moving. And the science backs her up on that. Studies have shown that low-impact exercise like walking and biking can help reduce the symptoms of arthritis. When she was ninety-three, Mom still enjoyed an active lifestyle and even shared her adventures—including paragliding and zip-lining—through public speaking and on social media.

She was constantly asked, "What's your secret?"

"If there's one thing I do pretty consistently," she'd say, "it's stretching."

When she was in her eighties, Mom's doctor advised her to limit one of her favorite exercise activities: jump roping. He said jumping on hard surfaces had him concerned about micro-fractures in her spine. She agreed but wanted to find a suitable alternative, and after researching the subject, Mom was surprised to learn that osteoporosis and bone loss are not necessarily inevitable with aging and that the right exercise program could actually help strengthen bones. By strengthening our muscles, we give our joints more support, and the muscles help keep our body flexible and limber. The best exercises for this are weight-bearing, such as walking and dancing. They make your muscles work against gravity to keep you moving and help you improve balance. And better balance means less risk of falling, so Mom thought that sounded pretty good, too.

She was determined to stay flexible and limber, and when she learned that stretching muscles slowly is important to the prevention of injuries, she said that made perfect sense to her because she'd noticed that when dogs and cats wake from a nap, they stretch slowly and deliberately, gently elongating their spine and legs. Dogs stretch their legs, sitting back on their haunches, and cats are more prone to arching and rounding their backs. They're both good role models, and Mom kept them in mind when she came up with a daily routine, which her doctor approved.

Her routine started as soon as she woke up, even before she got out of bed. Here's how to do what she did:

- Start with ten sit-ups while still in bed.

- Roll over (still in bed) and hold a plank position for sixty seconds.

- Get out of bed, stand a few inches from the wall, stretch both arms up, palms flat against the wall, and count to twenty.

- Get down on your hands and knees for dog and cat stretches. For the dog stretch, place both palms flat on the floor, keep your arms straight, and look up, stretching your arms and abdomen. For the cat stretches, round and arch your back. Start on your hands and knees on the floor. Bend your elbows and rest your forearms on the floor, palms flat. Lower your head toward your hands, gently stretching your back. With practice, you'll be limber enough to touch your forehead to the floor between your forearms.

- Finally, stand up and stretch your hamstrings by touching your toes—or getting as close as you can get without straining.

The Microwave Hop

Mom thought the kitchen was a perfect place for exercise. I got used to walking into the kitchen and seeing her hopping and humming while she waited for the microwave to beep. She said it was the perfect way to fit in some mini-movement sessions, ranging from thirty seconds to three or four minutes, depending on what she was cooking or heating.

The "microwave hop" was her signature kitchen dance no matter whose home she was in. A quick hop on both feet, followed by hopping from one foot to the other, prancing in place. If she had the time, she'd move on to her leg strengthening, lightly grasping the back of a chair for balance and standing on one foot while she counted to twenty, then switching to the other foot for another count to twenty.

She knew that grip strength was one of the tests doctors use to measure muscle loss, so she kept several hand-strength exercise balls on her nightstand and squeezed them while she read through social media postings. I always got a kick out of seeing how surprised people were when she shook their hands. They'd often say something like, "Wow, you've got a strong grip there." They seemed to expect someone over ninety to have poor muscle tone and a weak grip, but she enlightened them. And sometimes she'd go so far as to entertain them by demonstrating her juggling skills, which also helped to keep her hands and arms strong in addition to maintaining dexterity, balance, and hand-eye coordination.

She loved to demonstrate her exercise routines and encouraged others to join in. "I've found that doing this has strengthened my bones, improved my breathing, and decreased stress on my joints," she'd say. "I have hardly any fatigue, and my muscles feel good." Nobody could argue with that!

Keep Taking Those Steps
move it or lose it

"You can't help getting older,
but you don't have to get old."
—George Burns, American comedian, actor, and musician

Before retirement, many of us were used to adding extra steps and movement to our days by taking the stairs instead of the elevator, parking farther away from the office, or walking a few blocks to lunch instead of driving. But in our homes, we usually arrange things for convenience and efficiency, which makes sense when home is a place for rest and relaxation.

However, as we get older and spend more time at home, it may be helpful to rethink the way we've set it up. Changing the flow of the kitchen and moving dishes or cookware to a different cabinet can easily add more steps to our day as we prepare meals and put away dishes and groceries. Another small thing we can do that will make a difference over time is to keep the remote control next to the TV instead of within arm's reach. Getting up to change the channel prevents us from sitting for hours on end.

See how many small changes you can make to incorporate more movement into all your indoor activities.

Exercise Leads to Longevity

Exercise is the number one contributor to healthy longevity, even if you don't start exercising until later in life. It improves heart health, strengthens muscles to lower the risk of falls, sharpens mental function, and encourages social interaction. Many studies substantiate the benefits of exercise, including one conducted in Sweden that found that just two and a half hours of brisk walking per week can add three to four years to our lives. By investing about twenty-two minutes a day in exercise, we can add more than a thousand days to our life.

Twenty-two minutes of activity can equal a walk around the block or a local park. Having a dog to walk a couple of times a day is a wonderful way to add activity and meet people. Mall walking is also a popular option because it's a safe, well-lit environment that's cool in the summer and warm in the winter, there are benches to rest on and opportunities for socializing, and many malls are served by public transportation.

If you prefer the outdoors, farmers markets, craft shows, and even swap meets are interesting venues to browse for twenty minutes. Parking farther away isn't just for the young folks, either. If you drive to a restaurant or a store, make an effort to park farther away from the entrance to give yourself a little more exercise.

Once you start moving, your body functions better, so you feel better physically and mentally. And making movement part of every day doesn't mean doing an intense workout routine—all movement benefits our over-all health and quality of life. But once you get moving, you may decide that it's fun to include something more challenging. Regardless of our age, we can find healthy levels of activity and, over time, increase the amount of exercise we do and the level of exertion.

Take George Abel, for example. According to the *Vancouver Sun* newspaper, George completed the Vancouver Sun Run 10K race seventeen times before he passed away in 2018. He earned the title of the eldest participant in 2015, when he was ninety-five, and not only finished the course but set the fastest time in the over-eighty division. He placed first the following year as well. In 2019, three generations of his descendants walked in his honor, keeping up the tradition he'd started.

And George isn't the only one. At 101, Fauja Singh retired from competitive racing after taking up the sport only ten years before. Over the age of ninety, he ran more than 235 miles in nine marathons. At seventy-six, Tom Gipson achieved the title of the oldest man to win Professional Rodeo Cowboys Association money at the Cheyenne Frontier Days rodeo. At fifty-seven, Laura Sophiea competed in four Ironman triathlons in a single year.

Gladys Burrill Ran was ninety-two when she completed the twenty-six-mile marathon in just under ten hours. She held the Guinness Book of World Records record as the oldest female to complete a marathon until 2015, when Harriette Thompson completed the San Diego Rock 'n' Roll Marathon. Harriette was seventy-four days older than Gladys had been when she finished the twenty-six-mile route in just under seven and a half hours.

At seventy-two, Oscar Swahn earned the distinction of being the oldest person to compete in the Olympics in 1920 and being the oldest medalist of all time, winning a silver medal in the double shot running deer contest.

It's never too late to start, and once you do, you're never too old to keep going. Remember the study from Sweden —increasing our activity for twenty-two minutes a day can add as much as a thousand days to our life.

What will you do with a thousand extra days?

THE CHALLENGE
ADD ACTIVITY TO EVERY DAY

"Lack of activity destroys the good condition
of every human being, while
movement and methodical physical exercise
save it and preserve it."
—Plato

When we talk about being active, we often think of physical fitness or exercise. It can seem like a chore, a task we postpone for as long as possible. But movement is less strenuous while still being very beneficial. Practice being active just by adding a little more movement to your daily routine. How can you do more?

CHALLENGE CHECKLIST

(check with your doctor before starting any level
of new exercise or physical activity routine)

☐ Start each day with a stretching routine.

☐ Create your own version of the microwave hop.

☐ Return a shopping cart to the building instead of the cart return.

☐ Move the television remote across the room.

☐ Try chair yoga.

☐ Join a walking or exercise group.

☐ Make a plan for twenty minutes of activity a day.

☐ Add extra steps to your cleaning routine by vacuuming a room twice.

☐ Walk to the mailbox or down the block twice a day

☐ Rearrange a closet or the kitchen to make it less convenient.

☐ Park farther away from a store entrance in a parking lot.

☐ On driving trips, stop every few hours and walk for ten minutes.

15

Try Something New

a year in the life
of a nonagenarian

"Don't count the days.
Make the days count."
—Muhammad Ali, American boxer

We can decide to have a life filled with ordinary adventures. We don't have to spend a lot of money—many activities are free. We don't have to be in prime physical condition, and we don't even have to travel, although I highly recommend it. We can be bold, be home-town tourists, taste life, and never stop learning. And it's not difficult. All we have to do is decide to be open to the world around us and embrace life.

My mom always had a passion for life. She was interested in everything around her and always wanted to learn and explore. She always said it was in her blood—as an Icelander, her curiosity and desire for adventure came from her Viking ancestors. So it was no surprise when she announced on her ninety-third birthday that she wanted to dedicate the upcoming year to doing something special. As a stroke survivor, she wanted to share a message of living life with vitality, no matter what a person's age is. She'd noticed that a lot of people didn't honestly appreciate the wonder of life or recognize the opportunity for fun in their daily routines, especially people who thought they were too old to have fun, and that sparked the idea of taking a year to show that no matter how old you are, you can try new things and have new experiences and adventures. So she committed to trying and sharing ninety-three new experiences before her ninety-fourth birthday.

People constantly told my mom that she was inspiring and that her energy was amazing, but she never thought she was special; she simply wanted everyone else to enjoy life as much as she did. Sometimes we look at someone else's life and think that person is amazing—we see what wonderful opportunities they've had or what marvelous talents they've been given—but it's difficult to put that spotlight on yourself, to think, "I am amazing." Mom was no different. Her life had been one of highs and lows, adventures, and blessings, as most people's are. The trick is to keep a positive attitude and focus on all the good moments in life.

• • •

We kicked off the "Never Too Old" year by celebrating her birthday on May 21 in Chicago with five of my siblings and extended family members. From there, Mom rode to Minnesota to visit with one of my sisters for a few weeks. She loved the small town of Winona and the beautiful scenery of the landscape along the Mississippi River. Most days she would read, visit the library, and sample restaurants in the area. On Memorial Day she had an unusual opportunity to witness a very special tribute, and it marked her first new experience of the year.

1 *Memorial Day ceremony—Wreath on the Water.* In the Wreath on the Water ceremony, the flowers are lowered into the water and set adrift in honor of those lost at sea. Mom wrote later that she was awed by the ceremony, watching as two sailors leaned over the sides of the boat and solemnly placed beautiful wreaths into the river and saluted as the arrangements floated away.

At the end of the month, I picked her up in Minnesota and we drove to St. Louis, where we boarded a direct flight to Iceland. The annual trip to visit family and friends in her homeland had been planned for months, and each year we managed to fit in unfamiliar places and activities and revisit some of her old favorites.

2 *LAVA Centre, Hvolsvöllur, Iceland.* This newly opened museum and educational center offers an inside look at volcanoes, lava, and magma. The displays allow you to "see" how volcanic eruptions happen and how land is formed. We spent hours there because it was as fascinating as it was fun.

3   *Ice climbing.* Mom always wanted to explore an ice cave, so when the opportunity came up to go ice climbing, she immediately said yes. She'd stayed in touch with Gisli, her paragliding tandem partner, and when she called to book another paragliding adventure, he said he had a surprise for her: he'd arranged an ice climbing trip for her in an ice cave.

4   *Icelandic Roots/East Iceland Emigration Center, Vopnafjörður.* Vopnafjörður is a small village on the east coast of Iceland where my great-grandfather had a farm. Mom spent summers there when she was a girl, so we stopped there to visit some of her childhood haunts. It wasn't the first time she'd returned to her grandfather's farm and visited family, but it was the first time she visited the Emigration Center. On previous visits it had been closed, and she was thrilled to finally have a chance to look at the records and find more family members who emigrated from Iceland to other parts of the world.

5 *Skarðarströnd.* My grandmother Dagbjört, Mom's mother, had come from Skarðarströnd, but Mom had never visited the area. We took a full day to explore, visiting the village, the church, and the cemetery. Mom didn't know much about the family members who had lived there and loved the opportunity to learn about them.

6 *Television interview.* This was a major first. A reporter from the local television station, Ríkisútvarpið, or RÚV, had reached out to Mom about a project featuring Icelandic women who'd met foreign servicemen stationed at Keflavik during World War II. It was seventy-five years since the occupation of Iceland, and Mom had been among those who became war brides. After the reporter talked with her, though, she realized that instead of being limited to a single interview, Mom's whole life story would have appeal to the station's audience. So she became the subject of a different television show, one they called *Aldrei of Seint (Never Too Late),* that focused on her vitality and zest for living.

After ten days in Iceland, we returned to Illinois, and Mom settled into her routine of writing, daily walks, afternoons on the deck, and the occasional coffee and ice cream at the riverfront. And she also managed to have a couple of new experiences.

7 *Dinner with a stranger.* One day after attending church, Mom decided to take herself out to lunch at Cracker Barrel. When she requested a table for one, a gentleman standing nearby said he was also waiting to be seated and suggested they share a table. In true Mom fashion, she said yes. Afterward, she said having lunch with a total stranger ended up being a lovely new experience.

8 *Podcast interview.* Ilana Landsberg-Lewis, host of the podcast Grandmothers on the Move, invited Mom to be a guest on her show. When Mom called me to find out what a podcast was and ask if she should say yes, I said, "Absolutely!" She had a wonderful interview with Ilana, sharing her strategy of staying active and enjoying life no matter what your age.

In late June, shortly after the podcast interview, Mom headed back to my sister's house in Minnesota, where she'd be closer to several of her grandchildren and get to spend time with two of my sisters.

9 *Witnessing of record for Guinness Book of World Records.* J.R. Watkins, a manufacturer of health remedies, baking products, and household items, based in Winona, Minnesota, celebrated its 150th anniversary with a big goal: to break the world record for the greatest number of layers on a layer cake. And it succeeded. The cake measured just over six feet tall and had 260 layers—30 layers more than the previous record-holder. The folks from the Guinness Book of World Records were on hand to make the assessment, and Mom was there to witness it. Even better, she got to eat a slice of that record-breaking cake.

10 *Wine and cheese.* Mom attended her first wine and cheese festival. While she enjoyed the new flavors, she said her favorite part of the festival was the band and the music it played.

11 *Tasted avocado.* Technically a berry, avocados are considered a vegetable by most Americans. Mom gamely tried this "veggie" but definitely didn't like it.

CHAPTER 15: Try Something New   **201**

In August, Mom boarded a plane to Colorado to visit with one of my brothers and his wife. From there, they drove to Arches National Park to meet one of my sisters in Utah. The trip provided the perfect opportunity for both planned and spontaneous new experiences—seven of them, to be exact.

12 *Colorado Springs Airport.* After many years of traveling to Colorado using the Denver airport, Mom visited the Colorado Springs Airport for the first time.

13 *Cheyenne Canyon-Helen Hunt Falls.* They hiked to Helen Hunt Falls, a waterfall in North Cheyenne Canyon Park, located a short distance west of Colorado Springs.

14 *Hoosier Pass/Continental Divide.* On the way to meet up with more family members in Moab, Utah, they stopped at the Continental Divide in Colorado. Over the years, Mom had crossed the divide in several places but never stopped. This time she stopped and marked the occasion with a photo.

15 *Dining at Red Cliffs Lodge.* It was Mom's first visit to the Red Cliffs Lodge, and she was charmed by the replica of an outpost and its old-time cowboy setting. It was an opportunity for nine family members to get together for dinner and even celebrate a birthday—a first-time experience combined with a well-loved tradition.

16 *Deadhorse Point State Park.* Mom and her group enjoyed a short hike, admired the view, and marveled at the sad story of how the spot got its name. Cowboys used the spot as a corral for wild mustangs, fencing them in with available tree branches. On one occasion, for a reason no one knows, the horses were left at the spot without water and died of thirst within sight of the Colorado River.

17 *Safari tour in a Hummer.* The highlight of the Moab trip was the Sunset Safari Hummer tour from the Moab Adventure Center. Mom loved riding in the Hummer as much as she loved the tour.

18 *Arches National Park-Sand Arch Trail.* Mom had wanted to see Sand Arch Trail firsthand ever since she got a new computer a few years earlier and it featured an image of the park in its standard wallpaper slide show. She was thrilled to finally be able to do it.

After Moab, Mom stayed in Utah for a couple of weeks to visit with her children and play with her great-grand-children. Of course, they made time for a few new experiences.

19 *Red hair.* My father once joked that Mom had been a brunette when they met, was later a blond, and then silver-haired. The one hair color she'd never sported was red, so Dad had fun teasing her by innocently flirting with the redheaded nurse who cared for him during his cancer treatments. Although it was four years later, Mom decided it would be fun to be a redhead.

20 *Snowbasin Ski Resort.* Mom was excited to visit the site of the 2002 Olympic games. She said the area was gorgeous, lunch was fun, and the resort brought words like opulence and luxury to mind.

21 *3-D movie.* In Lehi, Utah, a normal afternoon outing turned into another first-time experience. The Museum of Ancient Life had exhibits of dinosaurs and ancient marine life and offered a 3-D movie of what Mom referred to as "critters in the ocean." The movie was, in her words, "intimidating and terrifying."

By the time Mom returned to Minnesota, autumn was settling in. The leaves were starting to turn, and she loved how it changed the Mississippi River scenery. There was a family wedding to focus on and lots of errands to complete, but she still found time to note a couple of new experiences.

22 *Kohlrabi.* While accompanying one of her granddaughters to a local farmers market, Mom spotted something that looked similar to a head of cabbage but was black. The vendor offered her a taste, and she took a cautious nibble. Her verdict: "Nope, I do not like it all."

23 *Halloween costume.* After living in the United States for over seventy years and raising ten children, Mom finally dressed up for Halloween for the first time, donning a cute pointy witch's hat to pass out candy in.

In December, Mom flew from Minnesota to Florida for a visit with one of my brothers and his wife. They planned a few things to help Mom out on her quest for ninety-three new experiences, but a few unplanned ones popped up, too.

24 *Lightning from an airplane.* It was snowing when they took off from Minneapolis and the pilot flew above the storm, allowing Mom to look down on an enormous billowing black cloud that made a crisp background for bolts of white lightning. The amazing sight even lasted long enough for her to snap a few photos.

25 *Seeing wild turtles.* At my brother's house, which was located in a neighborhood with lots of wildlife, Mom watched from the patio as a large turtle meandered across the lawn, drawing zero interest from the deer that were also in the yard.

26 *Interaction with deer.* Mom couldn't resist crossing the lawn herself to come within petting distance of the near-tame deer.

27   *Cirque du Soleil.* Mom and my sister-in-law took a day trip to Miami to see the Cirque de Soleil ice show. Mom had seen the Ice Capades before, but this was a completely new experience.

28   *Jupiter Island.* Two of Mom's favorite things—a lighthouse and a trail to explore—made her first trip to Jupiter Island fun and memorable.

29   *Manatee.* As they drove north from Miami, Mom spotted a sign for Manatee Sanctuary Park. Never having seen a manatee before, she of course insisted that they stop to check it out.

The following week, my oldest sister drove from Illinois to Florida and picked Mom up for a special trip. They headed to South Carolina to meet my sister's newest grandchild and made a few stops along the way.

30   *Lobster baked potato.* Food is an easy area for having new experiences, and this one didn't disappoint. "My favorite food is loaded baked potato and just about any seafood," Mom said afterward. "When you put them together—pile lobster on a potato? Wow!"

31 *Fort McAllister.* At this historic site, Mom heard stories from the Civil War, enjoyed the beautiful park, and found more trails to explore.

32 *Savannah, Georgia.* Mom and my sister had a full day to explore this town that neither had visited before. Mom was especially excited to visit the Ships of the Sea Maritime Museum, which she'd read about in a brochure.

33 *Trolley ride.* There aren't too many trolleys around, so when they found one in Savannah, it was the perfect opportunity to experience another first.

34 *Fort Sumter Educational Center.* Mom had heard of this fort where the Civil War started and was thrilled to visit it in person.

After their family visit, complete with a five-generation photo, my Mom flew to Arizona, where she joined me for the remainder of the winter. She arrived December 23, just in time for the big day.

35 *Arizona Christmas Team Roping.* For Mom, Christmas had always included snow and large family gatherings. This year it was filled with cacti, warm sunshine, and cowboys.

36 *Ten kids, nine states, two countries.* Reflecting on 2018, Mom realized she'd had an unplanned first: she'd visited all ten of her children at their homes—across nine states and two countries—in the same year. Usually, that type of travel spread across more time, or some visits were at her home.

37 *Southern New Year's traditions.* Our Alabama-born neighbor invited us over for a traditional Southern New Year's Day dinner. She explained that you eat black-eyed peas for their power to bring good luck and collard greens because they're green like money and will ensure a financially prosperous new year.

38 *Coyotes' howl.* Mom had read many books about early frontier life in America, but this was the first time she heard coyotes howl in the night. "Very spooky," she said. "I can't begin to describe the sound, but the effect on me was nerve-racking."

39 *Rock Springs Café.* An afternoon drive with my brother included a stop at a quaint café for pie and coffee. It turned out that the Rock Spring Café has the claim to fame of being the oldest independently owned restaurant still operating in Arizona. And the pies are wonderful.

40 *Jail Tree, Wickenburg, Arizona.* Without a proper jail, early law enforcement would chain offenders to a tree instead of a jail cell. Today, tourists can have a photo taken "incarcerated" at the tree. Of course, Mom took advantage of the opportunity.

41 *Juggling oranges.* While in Wickenburg, she came across a tree growing next to the sidewalk, heavy with ripe oranges, and she couldn't resist the opportunity. Mom plucked a few off a low branch and showed off her juggling skills. How often would she get a chance to do that? At least once!

In January, Mom flew to Texas for a week to visit with her two sisters, the first time the three of them had been together in nearly fifty years. They had each immigrated to the United States after World War II and had visited each other separately, but never all together.

42 *Lake Travis, Texas.* A nice condo with a nice view of a beautiful lake in Texas Hill Country.

43 *Sisters getaway.* Getting together with her sisters for a girls vacation was something none of them had ever done. All of them were over ninety years old when they experienced this first!

44 *Petting a rhinoceros.* The trio had an opportunity to visit TDS Exotic Wildlife Ranch, and Mom was able to interact with lots of animals—and pet a rhinoceros for the first time.

45 *Photographing a lizard.* Mom had never taken a photo of a lizard, so after she caught up with one and snapped the picture, it made her list of firsts.

46 *Petting a pig.* Who even thinks about petting a pig? Mom did.

After returning to Arizona, Mom took advantage of the warm weather and the many activities in the Phoenix area over the next few months.

47 *Throwing a lasso.* After spending time at the ranch and watching countless hours of team roping, Mom wanted to see how hard it was to learn. She put in a few hours to learn the basics and was actually able to lasso a practice dummy.

48 *Massage.* Mom had never considered getting a massage before, but once she started focusing on finding new experiences, she realized it was another perfect first.

49 *Crocheting/knitting.* While it wasn't the first time she'd learned to crochet or knit, Mom wanted to see if she could remember. It had been more than sixty years since she used the skill, and she was thrilled to find that the knowledge was still there when she picked up the needles and yarn.

50 *Sushi.* Mom wasn't impressed. "Okay, so I tried sushi," she said. "Thanks, I'll pass."

In March, Mom and I drove to Yuma, a couple hours' drive, for a Scandinavian festival. It was a nice road trip, and the weekend brought her five firsts.

51 *Yuma, Arizona.* Her first time visiting the southern Arizona town.

52 *Carrying the Icelandic flag.* Mom carried the Icelandic flag in the opening ceremony of the festival. It was an emotional experience, her first time marching and representing her home country at such an event.

53 *Chicken Dance.* Mom had fun flapping her arms, getting the hang of the dance moves.

54 *Norwegian dance.* The Norwegian dance proved easier to learn than the Chicken Dance, as it was similar to what Mom remembered from her childhood in Iceland.

55 *Territorial Prison, Yuma.* We read about the prison in a tourist brochure and stopped by for a visit before we left town.

The final six weeks in Arizona were enjoyable but busy. Mom had set a personal target of ninety-three new experiences and was behind in the count. She needed to have nearly one experience a day in order to make her goal before her birthday on May 21.

56 *New fast food.* We all fall into habits sometimes, and Mom was no different. McDonald's was her favorite go-to fast food restaurant, but she made a point to break out of that rut to try something completely different. She wasn't sure what El Pollo Loco served when she pulled in, but it turned out to be a tasty new experience.

57 *Driving a four-wheeler.* We have a four-wheeler on the property and room to drive around, so why not? Mom took it for a spin with our happy yellow Lab at her shoulder.

58 *Ordering from a food truck.* The perfect opportunity for an impromptu picnic while trying more new foods.

59 *GO-LIVE on Facebook.* Mom had texted, blogged, and posted on Facebook, but the video go-live feature was something new.

60 *Adult coloring book.* She'd colored pictures with her children years before, but the complicated designs found in an adult coloring book were a new experience and a challenging one.

61 *Inversion table.* My husband had used an inversion table to calm sciatic nerve pain, and Mom insisted on trying it out. She flipped upside down and said it made her back feel great.

62 *Homemade lemonade.* It was Arizona and we had access to lots of lemon trees—the perfect opportunity to make lemonade from scratch. Mom had never tried it before, and it was a delicious experience.

63 *Lake Pleasant, Arizona.* The lake is nearby, and it was the perfect destination one sunny day. After weeks of being in the area, Mom finally visited this lovely spot.

64 *Chair yoga.* Mom found a local senior center offering single-session chair yoga. She'd read about yoga and was eager to try it. She found that it was a great workout and a lot of fun.

65 *Hoverboarding.* The opportunity came up to try a hoverboard—with a sturdy seat attached—and Mom was soon speeding around the yard with a huge grin.

66 *Country line dancing.* A local country bar offers line dancing lessons every Friday night. It always looks like fun, so we decided to participate one week. Mom even donned new cowboy boots for the occasion.

67 *Reykjavik artist exhibition at the Phoenix Art Museum.* Mom was thrilled to see an Icelandic artist being featured at the Phoenix Art Museum in an exhibition called "Ragnar Kjartansson: Scandinavian Pain & Other Myths."

68 *Stealing a stranger's coffee.* Not every new experience is good, and some are a little embarrassing. In this case, Mom inadvertently grabbed another woman's cup at a coffee shop. She may have gotten away with it except that after a quick gulp, she gave herself away. "Yuck, they put sugar in my coffee!" she said. The lady next to her laughed. "You took *my* cup."

69 *Classic car museum.* Mom loved classic cars and often stopped to admire them when she spotted them parked somewhere. A full museum of classic cars was a treat, and after she discovered one in the Phoenix area, she paid a visit.

70 *Virtual reality.* When Mom found an online coupon for a virtual reality experience, she wasn't sure what it was but bought a session anyway. The drone-footage video let her travel the world in under an hour—including a stop in her beloved Iceland!

71 *Hole in the Rock.* A nice moderate hike and a great photo opportunity.

72 *Glass blowing.* Another activity found through online coupon shopping, the glass blowing class was interesting and even resulted in Mom's creating a birthday gift for one of her great-grandchildren.

73 *Mimosa.* On Mom's last day in Arizona, we marked the occasion with brunch, and Mom tried a mimosa—orange juice and Champagne.

In April, Mom flew from Arizona to Seattle to spend several weeks visiting my sister there and one of my brothers who lived across the border in Vancouver.

74 *10K-Vancouver Sun Run.* Mom's first run/ walk of any kind was canceled due to hail shortly after it started. Quite a memorable first!

75 *Presentation with an interpreter.* Mom often spoke to groups about a variety of topics, but working with an interpreter was new.

76 *Lutefisk.* More food experimentation! She loved many types of fish but it turns out lutefisk was not one of them.

77 *Watching herself on TV.* After nearly a year in production, the television special about her life that had been filmed in Iceland months before was finally aired. It was something few people get to experience: watching themselves featured in an hour-long TV program. Since it was on Icelandic television, she watched through a special Internet link.

78 *Skagit Valley Tulip Festival.* Mom was visiting Seattle at the perfect time of year to attend this annual festival.

79 *National Nordic Museum.* This stop had been on Mom's list for a while. She followed the museum's events through its newsletter and was thrilled to finally visit in person.

80 *A kiss and a serenade from a stranger.* After a presentation at a retirement home where she talked about her goal of ninety-three new experiences, a gentleman asked if she'd ever been serenaded. When she said no, he sang "The Rose" to her and gave her a kiss on the cheek.

81 *Kayaking.* My sister is an avid kayaker and helped Mom with another new experience: kayaking on Lake Union.

82 *Ethiopian restaurant.* Still more food experimentation! It was a bit spicy for her taste, but she was game to try a few dishes.

83 *Electric Slide.* She learned this new dance at the local senior center.

84 B*olivian restaurant.* Still more food experimentation! She said this cuisine was a little spicy but quite tasty.

From Seattle, Mom flew back to Minnesota, ready to home-base from there for the summer. However, my sister had recently accepted a new job and found out she would be moving from Minnesota to Iowa. Mom was excited at the opportunity to explore Burlington and then head back to Minnesota.

85 *Burlington, Iowa.* A visit to a new town.

86 *Walking Snake Alley.* A crooked, winding street named in "Ripley's Believe it or Not" as #1 Odd Spot in the 2017 Odd Spots across America Campaign.

87 *Driving an end loader.* Someone asked if she wanted to play in the dirt with a big truck, and she jumped at the opportunity.

88 *Wearing suspenders.* It wasn't a fashion trend she ever thought she'd join, but a belt wasn't enough to keep her jeans in place, so she gave them a try.

89 *Laser tag.* For her first time trying this game, Mom was joined by two granddaughters and their boyfriends, as well as my sister and her husband.

90 *Escape room.* Mom joined several family members to try an escape room, where you're locked in and have to follow clues to find the key and get out.

91 *Ball pit playroom.* At dinner one evening, Mom and one of her granddaughters explored the restaurant and were thrilled to find an adult ball-pit playroom upstairs. They jumped right in to the room full of multi-colored plastic balls.

As a proud member of the Icelandic community, Mom looked forward to the National Convention for the Icelandic National League of North America. I picked her up in Minnesota, and we headed north to Winnipeg, Manitoba.

92 *World's largest prairie chicken.* Driving by the sign on the interstate, who wouldn't stop if you haven't seen it before—let alone the world's largest?

93 *Meeting the president of Iceland.* Knowing that President Guðni Thorlacius Jóhannesson would be speaking at a convention we were attending, Mom's greatest wish was to meet him and have a photo taken with him. She was able to do just that less than a week before her ninety-fourth birthday.

THE CHALLENGE
TO LIVE

> "To live is the rarest thing in the world.
> Most people exist, that is all."
> —Oscar Wilde, Irish poet, author, and playwright

Living a full life means something different to each one of us. Spend some time thinking about what makes you smile, what makes you feel good. What makes you feel alive? Whatever your answer is, make it a part of every day. But above all, experience life through new experiences. Don't settle for a boring routine without surprises. Challenge yourself to try something new, big or small. It doesn't matter what it is—just stay open to new things.

CHALLENGE CHECKLIST
What Will Be on Your List?

☐ _____

☐ _____

☐ _____

☐ _____

☐ _____

☐ _____

☐ _____

☐ _____

☐ _____

☐ _____

☐ _____

☐ _____

☐ _____

☐ _____

☐ _____

☐ _____

☐ _____

☐ _____

"Enjoy life. There's plenty of time to be dead."
—Hans Christian Andersen,
Danish author of *The Little Mermaid* and *The Ugly Duckling*

Resources
add your favorites!

Blogs

- Blogarama
  Website: www.blogarama.com/en/

- Evelo-recommended blogs for seniors
  Website: www.evelo.com/blog/the-ultimate-
  list-of-blogs-for-seniors/

_____

_____

Coupon Sites

- Groupon
  Website: www. groupon.com

- Living Social
  Website: www.livingsocial.com

_____

_____

Education & Learning

Local community colleges: The program might be called Lifelong Learning, Continuing Education, or Adult Community Programs

- Website: www.thepennyhoarder.com/save-money/ free-college-courses-for-senior-citizens

_____

_____

Event Listings

- Eventbrite
  Website: www.eventbrite.com

_____

_____

Games-Online

Website: www.arkadium.com/free-online-games

_____

_____

Genealogy Resources & Heritage Groups

- National Archives' resources for genealogists
  Website: www.archives.gov/research/genealogy

- Grandmas Project
  Website: grandmasproject.org
  Email: hello@grandmasproject.org

- Find specific organization by searching the
  nationality in conjunction with "heritage club"
  "society" or "heritage"

_____

_____

General

- Local chamber of commerce

- Visitor & Convention Bureau

_____

_____

Outdoor

- The Audubon Society

  Website: www.audubon.org

  _____

  _____

Party Planning Resources

- Locally:

  - Real Simple website: www.realsimple.com/
    holidays-entertaining/birthdays/childs-home-
    birthday-party-checklist

  - Parents.com website: www.parents.com/fun/
    birthdays/ideas/the-perfect-kids-birthday-party

Senior Groups

- AARP

  Website: aarp.org

  Phone: (888) 687-2277

  _____

  _____

Social Media

- Facebook (www.facebook.com)

- Instagram (www.instagram.com)

- Twitter (www.twitter.com)

- LinkedIn (www.linkedin.com)

_____

_____

_____

_____

Technology

- FitBit

- Smartwatches

- Garmin

- Vivosmart

_____

_____

Ticket Services

- Ticketmaster

- Goldstar

- Eventful

Travel

- Department of Transportation Scenic Byways
  Program
  Website: www.fhwa.dot.gov/byways/

- Amtrak

- United States National Historic Landmark Program

- AAA

- Factory tours
  Website: www.factorytoursusa.com

Video Services

- Skype

- Zoom

- Facetime

_____

_____

Volunteer

- *Locally:* churches, community or senior centers, Veterans Administration, hospitals, library, animal shelters and rescue centers, food pantries, museums (website: www.wikihow.com/Volunteer-at-a-Hospital)

- Senior Corps
  Website: www.nationalservice.gov/programs/senior-corps

- Find a Need: www.nationalservice.gov/programs/senior-corps/get-involved/senior-corps-pathfinder
  National Service Hotline: (800) 942-2677

- U.S. Department of Veterans Affairs volunteer service
  Website: www.volunteer.va.gov

- Feeding America (food bank)
  Website: www.feedingamerica.org/take-action/volunteer

- Generations Unlimited
  Website: www.gu.org

- AARP's Foundation Experience Corps (reading)
  Website: www.aarp.org/experience-corps/experience-corps-volunteer

- National Park Service
  Website: www.volunteer.gov

- Musicians on Call
  Website: www.musiciansoncall.org

- The Federal Crowdsourcing and Citizen Science Catalog
  Website: www.citizenscience.gov/catalog

- Habitat for Humanity RV Care-A-Vanners
  Website: https://www.habitat.org/volunteer/travel-and-build/rv-care-a-vanners

_____

_____

_____

_____

_____

_____

_____

_____

References

"20 Reasons Why You Should Write Your Family History." Carmen Nigro, managing research librarian, Milstein Division of U.S. History, Local History & Genealogy, Stephen A. Schwarzman Building. New York Public Library blog. Posted February 9, 2015.

Kashdan, T, P. Rose and F. Fincham. "Curiosity and Exploration: Facilitating Positive Subjective Experiences and Personal Growth Opportunities," *Journal of Personality Assessment* 82:3 (2004); 291-305.

Institute of Education Sciences, National Center for Education Statistics. 2017 tables and figures, Table 303.40. "Total fall enrollment in degree-granting postsecondary institutions, by attendance status, sex, and age: Selected years, 1970 through 2027." https://nces.ed.gov/programs/digest/d17/tables/dt17_303.40.asp

"Nutritional Psychiatry: Your brain on food," Eva Selhub, MD, contributing editor. *Harvard Health Blog*, Harvard Health Publishing, Harvard Medical School. https://www.health.harvard.edu/blog/nutritional-psychiatry-your-brain-on-food-201511168626. November 16, 2015. Accessed May 12, 2020

"Eating more berries may reduce cognitive decline in the elderly." ScienceDaily. Wiley-Blackwell. www.sciencedaily.com/releases/2012/04/120426110250.htm. Accessed May 12, 2020

"Foods linked to better brainpower." *Healthbeat*. Harvard Health Publishing, Harvard Medical School. his: https://www.health.harvard.edu/mind-and-mood/foods-linked-to-better-brainpower. Accessed May 12, 2020

Arab, L., and A. Ang. "A cross sectional study of the association between walnut consumption and cognitive function among adult U.S. populations represented in NHANES." *J Nutr Health Aging* 19 (2015), 284–290.

Mercury News. "Sunnyvale museum docent celebrates historic birthday," Linda Kubitz. February 21, 2020

"Time spent in 'green' places linked with longer life in women." Elizabeth Pegg Frates, MD, contributor. *Harvard Health Blog*, Harvard Health Publishing, Harvard Medical School. https://www.health. harvard.edu/blog/time-spent-green-places-linked-longer-life-women-2017030911152. Posted March 9, 2017

Walch, J.M., B.S. Rabin, R. Day, J.N. Williams, K. Choi and J.D. Kang. "The effect of sunlight on postoperative analgesic medication use: a prospective study of patients undergoing spinal surgery." Department of Pathology, University of Pittsburgh. *Psychosomatic Medicine.* 67:1 (January/February 2005); 156-63

"The Cognitive Benefits of Interacting With Nature," Marc G. Berman, Department of Psychology, Department of Industrial and Operations Engineering, John Jonides, Department of Psychology, Stephen Kaplan, Department of Psychology and Department of Electrical Engineering and Computer Science, University of Michigan. Sage Publishing. https://journals.sagepub.com/doi/10.1111/j.1467-9280.2008.02225. December 1, 2008

Ryan, R.M., N. Weinstein, J. Bernstein, K.W. Brown, L. Mistretta and M. Gagné. "Vitalizing effects of being outdoors and in nature." *Journal of Environmental Psychology* 30:2 (June 2010); 159-168.

Kerr, J., S. Marshall, S. Godbole, S. Neukam, K. Crist, K. Wasilenko, S. Golshan and D. Buchner. "The Relationship between Outdoor Activity and Health in Older Adults Using GPS." *International Journal of Environmental Research and Public Health* 9:12 (December 2012); 4615–4625.

Jacobs, J., A. Cohen, R. Hammerman-Rozenberg, D. Azoulay, Y. Maaravi, and J. Stessman. "Going Outdoors Daily Predicts Long-Term Functional and Health Benefits among Ambulatory Older People." *Journal of Health & Aging.* April 1, 2008

Chicago Tribune. "What does the phrase 'young at heart' mean to you?" July 12, 2011.

Romundstad, S., S. Svebak, A. Holen and J. Holmen. "A 15-Year Follow-Up Study of Sense of Humor and Causes of Mortality: The Nord-Trøndelag Health Study." *Psychosomatic Medicine* 78:3 (April 2016); 345-353.

"Bone Health: Get the Facts." National Osteoporosis Foundation. https://www.nof.org/prevention/general-facts/. Accessed May 13, 2020

"Exercising with osteoporosis: Stay active the safe way." Mayo Clinic. https://www.mayoclinic.org/diseases-conditions/osteoporosis/ in-depth/osteoporosis/art-20044989. Accessed May 13, 2020

Moore, S., A. Patel, C. Matthews, A. Berrington de Gonzalez, Y. Park, H. Katki, M. Linet, E. Weiderpass, K. Visvanathan, K. Helzlsouer, M. Thun, S. Gapstur, P. Hartge and IM Lee. "Leisure Time Physical Activity of Moderate to Vigorous Intensity and Mortality: A Large Pooled Cohort Analysis." U.S. National Library of Medicine. National Center for Biotechnology Information. *PubMed.gov* https://pubmed.ncbi. nlm.nih.gov/23139642/. November 6, 2012. Accessed May 13, 2020

About the Author

Heidi Herman is an author of books in several genres, including women's fiction. *On With The Butter* is her first non-fiction work.

Her passion and a common theme in her writing is her Icelandic heritage. After releasing several children's books, in 2017, she co-authored a cookbook, *Homestyle Icelandic Cooking for American Kitchens* with her mother, Íeda Jónasdóttir Herman, which won a US category in The Gourmand World Cookbook Awards that year. Heidi's debut novel, *Her Viking Heart,* was named the 2018 Foreword INDIES Book of the Year Gold Winner, Romance Category.

Heidi was raised in Central Illinois but has made her home on a farm in South Dakota and spends winters in Arizona. In addition to writing, she loves cooking, photography, travel, and exploring the outdoors, pursuing adventure wherever she goes.

 www.facebook.com/heidihermanauthor

 www.Instagram.com/heidihermanauthor

website www.HeidiHermanAuthor.com

Other Books
by Heidi Herman

Women's Fiction

Her Viking Heart

Short Story Collection

The Guardians of Iceland and Other Icelandic Folk Tales

Cookbook (with Íeda Jónasdóttir Herman)

Homestyle Icelandic Cooking for America Kitchens

Children's Books

The Legend of the Icelandic Yule Lads

The Icelandic Yule Lads Mayhem at the North Pole

Read about Ieda's year-long
adventure of new experiences in

Never Too Late

Íeda Jónasdóttir Herman always believed you're never too old for something new. And, she thought that ordinary adventures were some of the best adventures. So, she set out on a mission to find ninety-three things she had

never done before and try them all between her 93rd and 94th birthdays.

The collection of the experiences are brought together in a new book, *Never Too Late.* Her stories and photos are presented in a journal-style memoir of that year.

Ieda had been working on the book when she passed away on October 9, 2019 and her daughter, Heidi Herman completed the inspirational work that proves you're never too old for something new.

Published by Hekla Publishing www.HeklaPublishing.com

Available from most online retailers and by special order from local booksellers.

CPSIA information can be obtained
at www.ICGtesting.com
Printed in the USA
LVHW030610170720
660909LV00002B/84

9 781947 233034